Work out – or work in?

Contributions to the debate on the future of work

Edited by Pamela Meadows

The **Joseph Rowntree Foundation** has supported this project as part of its programme of research and innovative development projects, which it hopes will be of value to policy makers and practitioners. The facts presented and views expressed in this report are, however, those of the authors and not necessarily those of the Foundation.

Contributors

Pamela Meadows is Director of the Policy Studies Institute
Bridget Rosewell is Joint Managing Director of Business Strategies Ltd
Patricia Hewitt is Head of Research at Andersen Consulting
Michael White is Senior Fellow at the Policy Studies Institute
Andrew Shaw is Research Fellow at the Centre for Research in Social Policy at Loughborough University
Ewart Keep is Senior Research Fellow at the Industrial Relations Research Unit, Warwick Business School
Ken Mayhew is Fellow and Tutor in Economics, Pembroke College, Oxford
John Philpott is Director of the Employment Policy Institute
Ed Mayo is Director of the New Economics Foundation

© Joseph Rowntree Foundation 1996

All rights reserved.

Published by YPS for the Joseph Rowntree Foundation

ISBN 1 899987 11 8

Prepared and printed by:
York Publishing Services Ltd
64 Hallfield Road
Layerthorpe
York YO3 7XQ

Cover photos: John Birdsall Photography

Contents

1 The future of work

Pamela Meadows

Introduction

The origins of this book lie in a seminar held in York in June 1995, sponsored by the Joseph Rowntree Foundation, which considered the likely pattern of work in the 21st century. The participants were drawn from a variety of backgrounds, disciplines and approaches, but all had been involved in some way in considering the future of work.

The chapters can be seen as stand alone papers – each has its own author – but the whole is worth considerably more than the sum of the parts. There are several themes that emerge time and time again:

- the change in the aspirations and status of women

- the shift from a collective to an individual perspective in many different aspects of life

- the desire for greater choice and autonomy

- the growing gap between those with jobs and all those without – including, but not only, the unemployed

- the change in the economic environment

- the change in the nature of the relationship between the economic and social dimensions of people's lives.

This overview chapter aims to capture those broad themes, and to provide some of the background which gave rise to the Foundation's original concern.

Background

The 1990s have been punctuated by pronouncements by gurus and journalists that the end of work is nigh. A thousand years ago, as the last millennium approached, there was an explosion in prophesies of apocalyptic events. One could argue that the labour market doomsters are no different from the other prophets of this millennium – from cults predicting the end of the world to the growing number of stories of abductions by aliens. But that would be a mistake. It is clear that a significant number of thoughtful and well-informed people are convinced that there is no longer enough work to go round, at least in developed industrialised countries – arguably there has never been enough work to go round in the rest of the world – and that this is not a temporary but a permanent problem. If true, this represents a major challenge to the way life has been organised in Europe and North America since the industrial revolution.

The Organisation for Economic Co-operation and Development set up its *Jobs Study* in 1992 as a recognition that high and persistent levels of unemployment represented a serious problem that was shared by nearly all the world's richest nations. It set out to examine the causes and the range of solutions that could be adopted. The European Union, with the publication of the Delors White Paper on *Growth, Competitiveness and Employment* in 1994 embarked on the same mission. As the Joseph Rowntree Foundation's Inquiry into Income and Wealth found, there is a close connection between not having a job and being in poverty. Furthermore, an important contribution to the changing income distribution between households is the changing pattern of employment and unemployment.

Unemployed people are increasingly found in households where nobody has a job. The proportion of working-age households with no earner has risen from 5 per cent to 20 per cent over the last 15 years (Gregg and Wadsworth, 1994). Such households are generally poor. That is not to deny that there are jobs that pay badly and that some of the poor are in work, but the single most important route out of poverty is to be part of a household where someone is employed. This means that the issue of whether or not work has a future is not just of concern to international organisations, national governments and futurologists. It matters to ordinary men and women.

It also needs to be stressed that although unemployment is a widespread problem in the developed world, its distribution in Britain differs from that elsewhere. In much of the rest of Europe unemployment is concentrated among young people and women who live in households where other people have jobs. This means that the unemployed are not necessarily, or even often, part of poor households. In the USA most unemployment is transitory and short-term, so that, again, it is not necessarily associated with continuing poverty and disadvantage. The concentration of unemployment in this country among men of all ages, and among the wives of unemployed men, has meant that we have a position where unemployment is closely associated with household disadvantage.

The economic context

Globalisation – in the sense of the transfer of production across national boundaries – was not a central feature of the discussion. However, the growth in production in less-developed countries, particularly those in Asia, is obviously a factor in the increasingly competitive environment confronting many companies (Wood, 1994). This is most apparent in the production of low-technology and low-skill goods and services. However, it is not new. Increased competition from international trade has been with us for well over a century. Indeed, it is arguable that it was more acute in the late 19th century than at any time since. There is no consensus in the wider debate, nor was there consensus at the seminar about the importance of this as a source of job loss.

Increasingly, sophisticated technology is tending to displace relatively routine functions, but it needs high levels of skill and knowledge to operate it effectively. Over the last 100 years the British education system has consistently failed to deliver the standards attained in other countries, except for the elite. As long as there remained a demand for unskilled labour this was not an insuperable problem. Now, when flexibility and adaptability are the key to successful performance, many of our workforce, particularly those whose experience has been confined to the Taylorist production lines of traditional British manufacturing, do not have the capacity to adapt.

Ewart Keep and Ken Mayhew demonstrate in Chapter 6, that what both globalisation and technological change have led to is not so much a loss in the overall number of jobs as an increase in the level of skill required in a whole range of jobs. Globalisation seems to be leading to international specialisation and, in international trade terms, developed industrial countries are having to specialise in high-technology, high-value-added sectors such as pharmaceuticals.

However, the seminar also considered those sectors of the economy where jobs are growing. One of the things many of them have in common is a strong emphasis on services involving personal contact – health care, hotels and catering, retailing and business services. There are obvious limits to the extent to which these can be delivered at a distance, although there is some international trade where the client goes to another country to receive the service there – university education being perhaps the best known example. The technical skill levels required in these jobs are often relatively limited, which is encouraging news for the unskilled. However, they do require the sort of interpersonal skills and the ability to work on one's own initiative that other employers are looking for.

A similar picture emerges for technology. Since the agricultural revolution of the 18th century, machines have replaced people in one group of functions but have generated opportunities in others. The ploughman has been replaced by the car mechanic and the farrier by the traffic warden. It is true that people have been displaced by computers. It is also true that one company, Microsoft, which did not exist 15 years ago, now directly employs 300,000 people in designing and selling software. Furthermore, many times that number are employed by retailers, specialist magazines, repair and maintenance services and in user support roles, to enable the product to get into the hands of consumers and to be genuinely useful to them.

Technology also has spinoff effects. For example, improvements in health technology have led to an ability to save lives, but complicated surgery and intensive care require high staffing levels as well as sophisticated equipment. Health technology has led to people living longer, but this means that a much higher proportion of the population survives into frail old age, which requires very labour-intensive care.

The social context

The economic and labour market developments discussed at the seminar have taken place against a background of, and interacted with, a number of powerful and sometimes related social trends. Perhaps the most important of these is the change in the position of women in society and in economic life. It is a recurrent theme in many of the chapters of this book.

Fifty (or even 30) years ago the majority of married women were economically inactive; lone mothers were predominantly widows, most of whom worked out of necessity; divorce was rare and expensive which largely confined it to the more affluent classes; single motherhood carried a social stigma which meant shotgun weddings in most cases, with most of the remaining babies being given up for adoption or abandoned; almost all young unmarried people of both sexes were economically active and virtually all men worked until retirement age.

If we take the household as the unit, 50 years ago the head of the household, whether male or female, was likely to be economically active, with other household members other than lodgers and adult or adolescent children likely to be inactive. This model, which had persisted since the industrial revolution, was envisaged by Beveridge as unchanging and still forms the basis of our social security system. However, it does not match present social reality.

The social institutions which supported the economic institutions of the 1950s and 1960s so effectively, are either showing signs of disrepair or have become irrelevant. As Andrew Shaw and Robert Walker discuss in Chapter 5, the benefit system, based on the male breadwinner model, makes it virtually impossible for partners or lone parents to retain or take up new jobs. Once they have been sucked into receipt of benefit it is very difficult to get out. This is due as much to the administration of the system as it is to its design. But as Patricia Hewitt suggests, at the other extreme, in families with two full-time earners there are signs that children are experiencing what she terms a parenting deficit.

Unemployment and inactivity

Many of the chapters in this book aim to help us understand how and why we are entering the 21st century with 7 million people of working age who have no jobs. Unemployment at less than 2 million is simply the tip of the iceberg. Increased participation of young people in full-time education is a healthy part of the explanation, but there is a growing tendency for men over 50 to stop working, and very few lone mothers have jobs. As Ed Mayo, Patricia Hewitt, and Andrew Shaw and Robert Walker all show, we live, rightly or wrongly, in a society where a job is what defines someone.

A century ago a rich man, particularly if he were a member of the aristocracy, would not dream of being anything other than a gentleman (or perhaps an army officer, which was a professional extension of the same thing). Even 30 years ago people felt quite comfortable describing themselves as 'gentleman' on their passports. Until the First World War married women rarely worked outside the home and, apart from wartime, it was not until the early 1960s that they started to work in significant numbers. Traditionally people were expected to have a job only if they needed the money. We now have the position where one of the sons of the reigning monarch works as a television producer, and he does so not because he needs to work to earn a living, but because it was deemed to be inappropriate for him not to have a proper job.

There has also been a shift in attitudes among women. Many of them now feel that a job of their own is an important part of their personal identity. Very few feel comfortable describing themselves as a 'housewife' – a description my own mother had as her profession on her passport even though she was in paid work for most of the time until she retired. Work is increasingly necessary for a social life. Members of extended families are less likely to live close to one another. The sort of domestic activities which women traditionally did collectively – washing and shopping being the most obvious – are increasingly done in isolation.

We now therefore have the position where most married women are economically active; many young people are in full-time education; the growing number of lone mothers from all social classes are mainly inactive and wholly dependent on benefits; half of all men over 55 are inactive and increasingly few men work until retirement age; and there are growing numbers of people who are drawing benefits because they are unable to work due to ill health or incapacity. There is no evidence that the average health of the population is declining at a rate that is consistent with this growth – if anything the opposite is true.

The numbers recorded as unemployed are outweighed by these other forms of inactivity, many of which seem to represent a withdrawal from a market within which it is difficult to compete, rather than genuine incapacity for any kind of work. But it is also likely to reflect the increased emphasis by employers on health standards in recruitment. It is notable that there is a close correlation between the geographical distribution of unemployment and the distribution of inactivity for health reasons (Schmitt and Wadsworth, 1994). There has been a redistribution of work from men to women, and from the old and the young to those aged between 25 and 50. Similar although not identical patterns are seen in other European countries. In particular, the shift from men to women has been especially marked in Britain.

Not all the reasons for these shifts are obvious, and neither are the underlying dynamic processes. It is not clear, for instance, whether we are seeing a change in the lifetime work patterns of quite large numbers of people, so that everyone has poor prospects when young and old but reasonable ones while in the prime age group, or whether particular individuals, who happen to be in a disadvantageous age group at a crucial point in the economic cycle, remain disadvantaged throughout their working lifetimes.

Inactivity is an important issue because it is work that generates wealth. Ed Mayo, in Chapter 8, reminds us that we need to recognise that the 'labour market' and 'jobs' are not the only way to think of or organise work. Nonetheless, it is essentially the wealth generated by those in our population who have jobs that is the source of the incomes of the remainder. This is true whether that income is derived from investments, an occupational pension, a share in someone else's earnings or social security. Non-market work does, of course, add to our national well-being, whether it is caring for dependants, volunteering, or non-monetary exchange schemes, and Ed Mayo's chapter gives an indication of the improvements that can be realised.

However, the difference between market and non-market work is that it is only in the case of market work that there are identifiable proceeds available for redistribution to non-workers. This redistribution comes in various forms, but the most important are taxes and dividends. Dividends are of increasing significance to a growing proportion of the population, since they are the main means of providing occupational pensions and more traditional savings instruments such as life assurance and endowment mortgages.

Harpo Marx was joking when he said that if work was so good why didn't the rich do it, but the joke has come full circle in Britain: it is the poor who do not have jobs and the rich who do. This has consequences for the distribution of income that are only now becoming apparent.

Customer choice

The chapters by Michael White, Bridget Rosewell, and Ewart Keep and Ken Mayhew reveal that there are factors in the economic environment that have led to a shift in the nature of the demand for labour. There has been a shift by consumers towards a preference for higher quality and more individually specified goods and services. In the days of Henry Ford, if you wanted to buy a car you could have a black Model T identical in every respect to every other Model T. Twenty years ago you got what the dealer had in the showroom – or what he had been allocated from the production line three months hence. Now, if you are prepared to wait a couple of weeks, your car will be built to order so that you get exactly the colour, trim and level of optional extras that you want.

People increasingly demand to be treated as individuals rather than be offered a standard product, and companies are having to respond accordingly. Many of the same issues have emerged in the area of public services – schools, hospitals and social services are the most obvious examples. The whole emphasis in the Citizen's Charter movement is on the right of the individual to have his or her own affairs and needs treated individually.

Competition has been introduced into areas where it did not exist before. With relatively few exceptions to date, this has had undoubted benefits for most consumers. It has turned many organisations which previously had a production-led focus towards a customer focus. But this has led them to scrutinise rather carefully exactly what everyone in the organisation does, and how they contribute towards satisfying the demands of customers. This has led to a preference for the employment of people who have good interpersonal skills and who are willing to place an emphasis on quality. It has also contributed to an upward shift in the occupational structure, although part of this is due to relabelling rather than any real changes – shop assistants being renamed sales managers or retail consultants, for example.

The employment relationship

As Michael White shows in Chapter 4, working relationships used to be governed by an implicit social contract. Most employers used to have some employees who were little more than passengers in economic terms, but who performed a useful social function. Often they were people who had originally been employed in jobs requiring physical strength, but who had subsequently become less able, through injury or age, to perform these kinds of tasks. There was an understood convention that certain categories of jobs were reserved for such people. Surface coal miners were traditionally former face workers. The job of lift attendant, for example, was reserved in law for disabled people. There were tea ladies, park keepers, railway station staff, street sweepers, bus conductors, messengers. It was recognised that many older workers had lower productivity than their younger colleagues and would have difficulty finding work with another employer, but they were valued for their experience and knowledge of how things really worked, and this could enhance the productivity of their younger, fitter but less experienced colleagues. Gold watches were not just tokenism, but a mark of genuine appreciation.

In the new competitive environment, individual items of costs are scrutinised closely and related to their contribution to output, sales or customer satisfaction. The economic environment has become riskier and employers have been passing that risk on to their workforces. The implicit social contract that governed working relationships has begun to break down. This contract was based on norms of behaviour; it was not based on regulation or other specific legal provisions. In spite of the rhetoric about labour market deregulation, there has been very little change in the regulatory regime as it relates to employer and employee, and both Michael White and Patricia Hewitt refer to this. There has, however, been a decided shift in the willingness of management to take advantage of the opportunities which the flexible legal framework in the UK allows. This is sometimes referred to as 'management's right to manage', but it seems to go deeper than that.

In the context of narrow financial measures of business performance, 'unnecessary' workers were eliminated first. Attention then turned to those who were 'not pulling their weight' or who had adapted insufficiently to the new environment. The social contract broke down surprisingly quickly, and did so in parts of the public sector as well as in the market sector.

As both Michael White and Patricia Hewitt show, the British labour market has never conformed to the full-time permanent employee standard. The lack of legal regulation has led to the development of a wide variety of working patterns – to a very large extent, until very recently, out of choice. There has been growth in part-time work over the 1990s, but the real growth happened during the 1970s. By 1980 part-timers accounted for 21 per cent of employees and by 1994 they had risen to 25 per cent. The growth in part-time work has been driven largely by the desire of many people to work less than full-time. Employers who want to recruit from this section of the labour force – women, students and older workers – have had to offer part-time jobs in order to attract them. Although in other western industrial countries there has been a growth in female labour force participation, elsewhere the growth has mainly been in full-time work.

Under 15 per cent of British part-time workers would prefer a full-time job. Part-timers are considerably more satisfied with their hours of work than full-timers, many of whom would like to work fewer hours than they do. However, more recently there have been indications that employers in some sectors, most importantly retailing, have started to prefer part-timers for business reasons. This is related to some extent to the extended opening hours in shops which mean that it is impossible for a full-time workforce to cover all the opening hours, and to changes in shopping patterns which produce peaks at weekends, evenings and lunchtimes. Other service industries which experience similar peaks and troughs are moving in the same direction.

Similarly, temporary or short-term contracts now cover around 7 per cent of employees – up from 5 per cent a decade ago. There does seem to have been a conscious move by employers to take greater advantage of the flexible regulatory regime and to consider at the point of recruitment whether they genuinely want or need a permanent full-time employee for a particular position. Caution, and a desire to minimise the amount of time not spent productively, has led to greater use of more flexible forms of contract for new recruits. However, since there has been little change in the incidence of such contracts in the overall population, it seems reasonable to conclude that many initially temporary jobs become permanent later.

In any case, the security of a permanent full-time job is not that great. Employers have the right to dismiss anyone on the grounds of redundancy or inadequate performance, and their horizons have become broader in terms of looking for people or functions that are unnecessary.

The central theme of Michael White's chapter is that the workplace itself has become a tougher and riskier environment. The heaviest burden of the new tendency towards risk sharing has fallen on those working in manufacturing industry, where the economic environment has been the most difficult, and on the less skilled, the sick and the otherwise disadvantaged. The better educated, more articulate, young and healthy, especially women, have had an increase in the choices and opportunities available to them, provided they could deliver on the new terms – show good interpersonal skills, flexibility, problem solving, team working and initiative. During the seminar, one of the participants described the process as 'Social Darwinism'.

But Ewart Keep and Ken Mayhew's account of employers' relatively low demand for skills in Britain by comparison with other industrial countries might reflect another dimension of companies' aversion to risk – keep it simple and stick to what you know. Employers seem to want good standards of general education and presentation skills, but it is not clear that they are yet seeking high standards of technical knowledge or ability. In the context of greater international competition, in this case from other developed industrial countries such as Germany, Italy and the USA, this strategy may not be as low risk as it appears to those who have adopted it.

It is also not yet clear whether the riskier work and social environment is now beginning to affect the group that has hitherto benefited from the opportunities provided by the new flexibility. One argument is that we now hear a good deal more about insecurity because it is affecting middle-class articulate men for the first time. The large increase in white-collar redundancy seen during the last recession is likely to have had an impact on expectations and attitudes. Opinion polls show that people perceive the labour market to be a risky place and fear of job loss pervades a much larger segment of the population than is genuinely at risk. It is one explanation for the current lack of a 'feel-good' factor and the consequent unwillingness to spend on housing or discretionary consumption. These in their turn have had a dampening effect on the overall economic recovery.

Social cohesion

This 'leaner and fitter' approach to employing people should be contrasted with that in Japan, where shops and restaurants employ people simply to open doors, greet people, and wrap or carry their parcels. This is reflected in their prices, but there is a strong social belief that people, especially men, should be usefully employed. Accountants would argue that such a system is highly inefficient, but that may only be true when viewed from a narrow perspective. A society with a high level of cohesion is likely to be less dysfunctional in many ways, although it is likely to be conservative and conformist as well (the employment in Japan of female graduates as 'office ladies' who greet visitors and make tea is a good illustration of this).

In Britain, there has been increasing geographical segregation of the poor, caused by the apparently sensible policy of concentrating social housing resources on those in the greatest need and encouraging those who can do so to provide for themselves. This has led to the concentration of disadvantaged families on council estates and to their increasing isolation from the rest of the community. Nearly half of all council tenant households of working age now have no earner (Schmitt and Wadsworth, 1994). The concentration of the incidence of unemployment in households where nobody has a job means that it creates greater social stress than it does in other countries where the unemployed tend to live with people who have jobs.

It has also become increasingly apparent that people who experience one disadvantage often also experience another. There are correlations between ill health and unemployment, for example, although the direction of causality is not completely clear. Those with less good health records may be more likely to become unemployed; but unemployment is a stressful experience and there are clear associations between stress and ill health. There is growing concern that the coincidence of multiple disadvantages is overloading the capacity of communities to police themselves and to socialise young people.

There may have been a growing polarisation between those who have access to transport, who increasingly live their lives partly within and partly outside their home areas, and those whose focus remains confined to a limited geographical area. The long-term economic and social consequences of this are likely to reach well beyond those most immediately affected. Once the full range of costs is considered, it is not clear that the Japanese approach is less efficient.

The purely economic focus of many interventions to help the unemployed ignores the fact that there are often several dimensions of people's lives where they are at a disadvantage. Part of their problem is that the different agencies only deal with a single dimension without taking account of the interactions. For instance, although it is increasingly rare for council tenants to have jobs, the job of the housing department is to deal with their housing problems in isolation and to ignore the rest.

John Philpott in Chapter 7 shows how, looking at the labour market in isolation, there is no such thing as a free lunch when it comes to reducing unemployment. Whichever approach is adopted has some net cost to the taxpayer. The challenge, which has not been fully addressed by anyone, is how far these costs might be justified by the improvement in the overall economic and social structures of communities, and therefore in their ability to reduce the level of their interaction with other public agencies such as the police, the health service and social services.

Recent research published by the Foundation (JRF, 1995b) has illustrated clearly how this problem affects young people. Schools will only deal with education issues; social services will deal with neglect and some behavioural problems; doctors deal with specific health problems; the criminal justice system deals only with crimes that have already been committed. If in addition the young person has a parent or parents who are dependent on benefits, that introduces yet another dimension of difficulty into their lives. A significant amount of taxpayers' resources may be being devoted to supporting an individual family, and yet none of the agencies has any interest in saving money for the others by taking stock of all the difficulties and trying to solve them in a constructive and interrelated way. The introduction of performance targets and the allocation of resources by objectives in the public sector, while in many ways a desirable move, has made it even more difficult than it used to be to justify expenditure which has its main beneficial impact on the operations of another agency.

The distribution of work

Over the last 20 years national output in the UK has grown by 45 per cent. There are some who find this hard to believe, because it does not accord with their own experience. This is largely because one remarkable feature of the UK labour market over the last 20 years has been the appropriation by those in work of much of the increased wealth that has been generated. While unemployment (and other forms of inactivity) have been on an upward trend, earnings have grown faster than inflation in virtually every year. As work by Tony Atkinson (1994) conducted for the Foundation's Inquiry into Income and Wealth has shown, within this average the earnings of those in the upper part of the earnings distribution have grown faster than those in the lower part. We have also seen an apparent growing unwillingness by the employed to pay taxes to support those who do not have jobs. This has added to the growing disparities between the incomes of those with jobs and those without.

It is important to stress that this process was not inevitable, and indeed was unusual among industrial countries. Other countries did not see the same widening of the income distribution nor the same rapid rise in real (after inflation) earnings as has occurred in Britain.

There is clearly a question mark here: is the problem really one of not enough work, or is it a matter of its distribution? Do some people have too much work and others too little? There is some evidence that men who were brought up in the expectation of doing manual work in manufacturing industry are not very willing to apply for what they perceive as 'women's jobs'. This puts them at a particular disadvantage given the shift from manufacturing to services that has marked the last 30 years or so. But it also helps to reinforce the cycle of exclusion.

If the only people who apply for service jobs are women, and half of them want only to work part-time, employers are forced to divide their jobs up into part-time parcels to attract any labour at all. This in turn excludes from consideration all those (particularly those on benefits) who can only afford to work full-time. As Michael White shows in his chapter, in southern European countries, and to some extent in France, men are willing to do 'women's jobs', and the women have much higher unemployment rates than men – the reverse of the UK picture.

Improving the competitive position of those without work by means of active labour market policies of one sort or another is desirable, for social justice and in terms of the cost to the taxpayer, but it does very little to improve the overall level of employment except at the margin, as John Philpott shows in Chapter 7. The main route by which it does so is by the faster filling of hard-to-fill vacancies, which increases the general level of economic activity. However, as Andrew Shaw and Robert Walker remind us in Chapter 5, it needs to be recognised that unemployed people receive few job offers because there are few jobs available. This is in contrast with the position in the United States where higher levels of job turnover generate a larger number of vacancies.

In the UK context it is difficult to argue for active labour market policies on grounds of anything other than equity. But this is complicated by the fact that there seems to have been a shift in perception by taxpayers that they are unwilling to pay for anything other than services from which they benefit, or potentially benefit as individuals. The Citizen's Charter notion of the citizen as consumer rather than as a member of a wider community has tended to reinforce this notion. But increased equity may be in the long-term interests of the more prosperous as well as those who benefit directly if it leads to a more stable social structure.

The conclusions of the seminar were necessarily tentative. Much of the jigsaw remains missing and the gaps have to be filled by inference. However, it was felt that there was a future for work, but there remained an underlying concern about work for whom. The new jobs created over the past 20 years have gone to groups of new labour market entrants – married women, students and those of independent means. The supply of these groups is by no means exhausted. Under half of all full-time students over 16 have jobs, and the proportion is much higher in the younger age groups than the older. There are both supply and demand factors that are likely to increase the student labour force participation rate, most notably the fall in the relative value of student support and the growth in weekend and evening shopping.

The labour force attachment of younger cohorts of women seems to be stronger than that of their predecessors. There are signs that a child-care industry like that seen in the USA is beginning to develop. The Government is encouraging the establishment of after-school care schemes, which are likely to increase the participation rate of mothers of primary schoolchildren. Currently participation rates rise sharply once children are in their teens. Female graduates already have participation rates very close to those of men, and although this may not be replicated across the board, since it is likely to reflect the fact that their earning power allows them to pay for child care and other domestic help, it does suggest that there is scope for further equalisation.

Attempts are being made to improve standards in education, but there remains a long way to go. Almost by definition, this improvement is concentrated among those currently aged under 16. For many years to come, the vast majority of the population of working age will have been untouched by any school-based improvements that might have been achieved. So the question is not really will there be work, but will there be work for those whose qualifications are limited or non-existent, or whose experience has not prepared them for work in the modern world. In the past, economic prosperity alone has enabled people deemed to be unemployable to find jobs and make a contribution to national economic and social life. For much of the 1960s total unemployment was around 300,000, and many of those were simply between jobs. The numbers who were deemed to be incapable of making an economic contribution were very small indeed.

Whether a period of sustained growth can lead to a return to that general position again in the future remains an open question. And within that question is the central one about the terms and conditions of employment, particularly the wages, which might be available to the least skilled groups. There are suggestions from some economists that their contribution to output is so far below prevailing wage levels that it will not be possible to secure them a wage which allows a reasonable standard of living without some form of subsidy (see, for example, Minford, 1994). We may need a blurring of the boundaries between work and non-work. A job, after all, before the industrial revolution used to mean a particular task, and the word is still used in this sense in domestic life. Everyone had an occupation. Sometimes they were practising it, sometimes not. The boundaries between work and the rest of life were fluid. Different periods of the past would lead to different conclusions, and there is no way of knowing which is the right one, but it is important not simply to be bound by current constructs, as Ed Mayo reminds us.

The future

The UK labour market is failing to distribute income and wealth to a significant minority of the population. This is neither inevitable nor necessary, as an overview of the experience of other countries will quickly show. There is and will continue to be a need for people to produce goods and provide services.

We may need to reconsider our views as to the suitability of different types of jobs for different types of people. Men may need to take 'women's jobs' and employers may need to reverse the shift towards part-time work. We need to recognise that many employers are discriminating against men. We have become so accustomed to the idea that the labour market discriminates against women, that we have simply failed to notice that in many areas the reverse is now true.

We need to examine the workings of the benefit system, both in terms of its rules and in terms of their administration, since it is increasingly apparent that they act as a major obstacle confronting those without work who want to work.

We might need to bring back a sense of shame. It used to be considered a sign of failure for a company to have to reduce its workforce. It is now, perversely, considered a sign of success.

None of these are technical economic issues. Indeed, the evidence suggests that we do not have a technical economic problem. Our growth rate over the past ten years or more has been good, both historically and in comparison with other apparently successful developed countries. Our record on growth of employment is well above the OECD average. We have a problem which is the outcome of a series of unrelated choices that have interacted with each other to produce an affluent majority and an increasingly impoverished minority.

Perhaps the most important thing we can do is to recognise that we have a problem which is not simply going to resolve itself by means of economic recovery. We have had a recovery that has generated quite high rates of output growth and a reasonable number of new jobs. Yet it has not really even scratched the surface of the numbers without work. This seminar recognised that unemployment is a challenge that confronts all of us.

References

Atkinson, A. B. (1994) *Seeking to Explain the Distribution of Income,* London School of Economics Welfare State Programme Paper 106

European Commission (1993) *Growth, Competitiveness and Employment,* CEC

Glyn, A. (1995) 'The assessment: unemployment and inequality', *Oxford Review of Economic Policy,* vol. 11, no. 1, Spring

Gregg, P. and Wadsworth, J. (1994) *More Work in Fewer Households?* NIESR Discussion Paper no. 72

Gregg, P. and Wadsworth, J. (1995) 'A short history of labour turnover, job tenure and job security, 1975–93', *Oxford Review of Economic Policy,* vol. 11, no. 1, Spring

Joseph Rowntree Foundation (1995a) *Inquiry into Income and Wealth,* JRF

Joseph Rowntree Foundation (1995b) *Multi-agency Work with Young People in Difficulty,* Social Care Research Findings 68

Minford, P. (1994) *The OECD Problem of Low Wages and Unemployment: The Role of Welfare Support,* University of Liverpool (mimeo)

Nickell, S. and Bell, B. (1995) 'The collapse in demand for the unskilled and unemployment across the OECD', *Oxford Review of Economic Policy*, vol. 11, no. 1, Spring

OECD (1994) *The OECD Jobs Study: Facts, Analyses, Strategies,* OECD

Schmitt, J. and Wadsworth J. (1994) *Why are 2 Million Men Inactive? The Decline in Male Labour Force Participation in Britain*, Centre for Economic Performance Working Paper no. 338

Wood, A. (1994) *North–South Trade, Employment and Inequality*, Clarendon Press

2 Employment, households and earnings

Bridget Rosewell

Introduction

This paper looks at the future of work in the context of likely and existing trends in the labour force and employment. There has been increasing concern recently that some groups of people are likely to be excluded from the labour market in future and will become, if they are not already, marginalised from society. This has wide implications not only for the future of work but also for social security, for crime and for society as a whole.

At the same time, in any economy, there are changes going on in the face of changing technologies and product-demand patterns. A solution to low pay and to poverty that flies in the face of these changes risks being unsuccessful or restrictive of wider opportunities.

This chapter looks at these issues in the light of the existing trends in the overall economy, what is happening to the workforce, what is happening to sectoral trends in employment, and what this means for household incomes. It also looks at how existing trends may change and the risk that patterns of development based on such trends can be both wrong and misleading.

The workforce

Trends in participation

Recent years have seen significant changes in the workforce – the number of people who are either working or who want to work. Indeed, it could be argued that this is as important a determinant of unemployment as the number of jobs available. Certainly, we will be unable to understand unemployment unless we also understand why people work. Individual motivation not only has a direct impact on work patterns but also interacts with the nature of households.

When Beveridge was writing, as has been shown in the Social Justice Commission report (1994), there was a fundamental assumption that workers were men. They lived in families, where women were responsible for home-making and domestic support, and most households also included dependants. The majority of men worked from the time they left school until retirement age.

While this stylised fact was probably always a simplification, it lay behind policy formation and work practices.

This stylised fact is no longer true. Nearly half the workforce is female and the length of time that any individual spends in the workforce has fallen. This is not just because of women moving in and out of the workforce, but also because of rising proportions entering higher and further education and retiring 'early'.

Table 2.1 shows the latest official projection for activity rates by age and sex. In 1971, over 90 per cent of men of working age were in the labour force, and just over half of women. It is predicted, based on existing trends, that 84 per cent of men and 74 per cent of women will be in the labour force by 2001: leading to a small rise in the overall proportion of the population who are in the labour force, but a substantial change in structure.

This means that in 1971 the labour force was 25 million people. By 2001 it is expected to be 28.7 million, but this is an increase of only one million on 1994 estimates. Forty-five per cent of these are likely to be women, compared to 36 per cent in 1971.

Males and females

The reasons for changing participation of men and women reflect a range of interacting factors. Work – that is paid work – has come to represent a whole variety of desirable characteristics during the 20th century. Perhaps chief among these is independence. Work gives an independent identity, income and justification. Though the work itself may be monotonous and badly paid, it may still be preferable to the isolation and dependence of the home. Surveys of women have consistently shown that the ability to make contact outside the home and a contribution to the household are powerful motivations.

Before the Second World War, homemaking was easily a full-time job in itself. The rise of domestic electrical equipment, smaller families, and more mobile communities breaking down older social relationships, have both enhanced the attractiveness of working outside the home and made it possible.

As the amount of time necessary for domestic tasks fell, the opportunity cost of doing other things also fell. This economic fact interacted with social changes – such as women's experience of working during the war and pressure for emancipation. It is worth remembering how recent some of these changes are. It was only in the 1930s that all adult women became eligible to vote, and the University of Cambridge only allowed women to receive full degrees in 1947.

Table 2.1 Estimates and projections of activity rates in Great Britain (%)

	1971	1981	1991	2001
Men				
16–19	69.4	72.4	71.4	58.0
20–24	87.7	85.1	88.5	81.1
25–34	94.6	95.4	95.9	95.3
35–44	96.2	96.0	95.7	93.7
45–54	95.7	94.8	91.6	90.2
55–59	93.0	89.4	80.8	74.6
60–64	82.9	69.3	54.1	52.8
65–69	30.4	16.3	15.2	14.3
70 and over	10.9	6.5	4.8	3.5
All ages	80.5	76.5	75.0	71.8
Working age	90.7	89.1	87.8	84.5
Women				
16–19	65.0	70.4	68.8	56.8
20–24	60.2	68.8	73.8	69.8
25–34	45.5	56.4	69.9	74.5
35–44	59.7	68.0	76.8	81.1
45–54	62.0	68.0	72.8	78.8
55–59	50.9	53.4	54.6	57.1
60–64	28.8	23.3	24.1	29.2
65 and over	6.3	3.7	3.1	2.8
All ages	43.9	47.6	53.2	55.7
Working age	56.7	64.0	71.2	73.6
All persons				
16–19	67.3	71.4	70.1	57.4
20–24	74.0	77.1	81.3	75.5
25–34	70.4	76.1	83.0	85.1
35–44	78.0	82.1	86.3	87.5
45–54	78.5	81.4	82.2	84.5
55–59	71.2	70.9	67.6	65.8
60–64	54.1	44.9	38.5	39.4
65–69	11.3	6.3	5.4	4.6
All ages	61.3	61.4	63.8	63.4
Working age	74.5	77.1	79.9	79.2

Source: Employment Gazette, *April 1995*

It is not surprising that the big changes in participation among women have happened in the prime age groups between 25 and 55. This reflects both changing attitudes among younger women and the opportunities available in new industries. These are also the age groups in which there has been least change for men. Over 90 per cent of men in these age groups worked in 1971 and only slightly smaller proportions are expected to be working in 2001.

Of course an analysis based on trends may be misleading. It may be argued that child-bearing responsibility will inevitably limit the ability in the main relevant age groups to continue working. On the other hand, if more widespread child-care facilities become available, then this participation could even increase. In countries with more readily accessible child care, there is certainly less difference between age groups than there is in the UK. Brannen *et al* (1994) show that the employment rate for women with children is well below the highest-level countries such as Denmark. Although the UK experienced one of the fastest growths of employment of mothers with children under ten between 1981 and 1991, this only served to bring the UK up to the EU average.

There could, of course, be a backlash in the future against women working, which would make it more difficult for them to get jobs. This seems unlikely, however. Employers will not want to lose this source of labour and women will not tamely submit to being forced out of the activity that provides income and gives independent shape to their lives.

Policy in this area will have to be developed with the acceptance that there is an increasingly even balance in participation rates in the labour force between the sexes.

The age effect

We showed above that it is in the prime age ranges that men's participation has fallen least and women's risen most. It would appear that work is being increasingly concentrated in the middle years, with falling participation for people under 20 and over 55. The change for the youngest age group is evident in the forecast rather than in the past. It reflects the sharp rise in the last few years in the proportion of young people staying on in education. It might be argued that this is a recession effect that will subsequently unwind. However, structural changes are likely to militate against this. These are of various kinds.

Notably, there is the advent of Training and Enterprise Councils, which not only administer the Government's Youth Training Schemes but are also charged with building Education–Business Partnerships and getting Modern Apprenticeships off the ground. Their standing and success reflect the success of getting training taken seriously. Further, there is the transmogrification of polytechnics into universities, and independence for colleges of further education. Both of these have meant an expansion of courses and an enormous marketing effort being put into further and higher education. There is much more competition between institutions for students, funds and status now that they are liberated from local authority control. The need for all these institutions to attract students is making young people increasingly aware of the importance of training and what is available.

The existence of targets for foundation learning is also pushing in this direction. This is not to argue here about the quality or relevance of much of the training: that is looked at elsewhere in this volume. It does, however, suggest that the shift in trend that has been apparent in the early 1990s is likely to continue. At worst, the higher participation rates in education will be maintained.

At the other end of the scale is the trend for earlier retirement. The arguments for a future break in trend are possibly as strong as those for young people, but the forecast at the moment builds on the past trends. Earlier retirement has up to now been largely market driven. With fewer jobs available in recession, and the pressure for restructuring workforces within companies, it has often been those at the end of their working lives who have been offered redundancy. There are two basic reasons why this might continue.

First, restructuring of work is still taking place, particularly among service industries where little happened during the 1980s. Many big companies – of which BT has been one of the most publicised – have removed or reduced layers of middle management and rationalised what is left. Achieving this has often meant making redundant numbers of staff who had been in position for some time. This process is still continuing, both in BT and in many other companies.

Second, there is a perceived need for accelerated change within business and for the acquisition of new skills, particularly computer-based skills. Rightly or wrongly, older workers are not viewed as being adaptable enough. They want to continue doing their jobs the way they have always been done, rather than seeing the benefits of change. At least at present, experience is not a valued commodity.

However, there are some arguments why this might change. First, in some areas at least, companies are discovering the benefits of older workers and focusing on them. In some DIY stores, older workers are being recruited as being more reliable and, in particular, knowing something about the product. What is more important, an increasing proportion of older workers will be those who not only embrace computer skills but who are also unwilling to retire at 55. Increasing longevity and health into the 70s may make many feel they do not want to be unemployed this long – especially if redundancy terms become less favourable.

Someone who will be 55 in 2001 was 25 in 1971 – in the midst of the white-hot heat of the technological revolution! Such people may be very different propositions from the person who was 55 in 1991 and 25 in 1961 when the post-war boom was at its height. Whether this is the case of course remains to be seen, but it is certainly a possibility.

The other pressure towards continued participation is financial. Though the most significant pressure on pensions will come well after the turn of the century, increasingly packages for early retirement may become less generous and more retirees will be concerned about financing their later years because of changes in social care provision for the elderly. Retiring in your 50s, with the prospect of another 30 years of life and possibly some heavy expenditure at the end of it, will not be an attractive prospect.

What does all this add up to? The official projections suggest that the size of the workforce will remain broadly stable, though it will be more balanced between males and females and biased towards prime age groups. The argument above suggests that, if anything, the workforce could be bigger. However, female participation is still constrained by child care, and older workers may not be willing to leave gracefully. If this is the case, it raises the question of whether there will be jobs for these people.

They can, of course, be forced out of the workforce – that is not be measured as part of it. Successive changes to unemployment statistics have already performed this statistical trick for some groups of people. In broad terms, however, if full employment means being able to work if you want to, then the measured labour force is only a part of the story.

We know that the workforce falls when unemployment rises, and people are deterred from looking for a job (*Employment Gazette*, March 1988). This does not mean that people would not start looking if they believed that jobs were available. Moreover, recent increases in unemployment across Europe seem to be driven more by increased demand for work than by a shortage of jobs (Glyn, 1995). Of course, it is also possible that people work when they would rather not and are forced into the labour force – for example when they would rather study or work fewer hours and spend time with their family. It is to these trends that we now turn.

Figure 2.1 Parents' employment at a family level

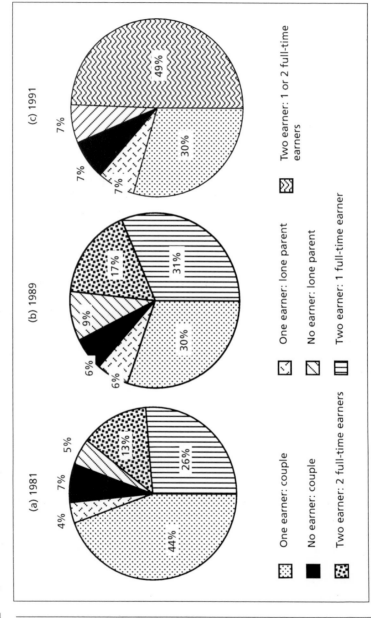

(a) 1981   (b) 1989   (c) 1991

Sources: (a and b) Labour Force Survey; (c) Dex, S., Clark, A. and Taylor, M. (1995) Household Labour Supply, Employment Department Research Series no. 43

Households

The two-earner household

Many of the changes in the labour force have happened to parents and have produced – against the earlier paradigm of the household consisting of two adults, of whom the man was the earner – the paradigm of the two-earner household and the single-person household.

In 1981, 23 per cent of households consisted of single persons. By 1991, the figure was 27 per cent and we expect this to rise to 31 per cent by 2001 (BSL Household Projections).

In 1981, 44 per cent of parents were in one-earner couples. By 1991 this was down to 30 per cent. The proportion of two-earner couples was up to nearly 50 per cent from just under 40 per cent a decade before (Figure 2.1). Of course, the majority have one of the earners working part-time. Even so, the proportions both of those with one full-time and one part-time partner, and of those with two full-time partners have grown (Dex *et al*, 1995).

This phenomenon is likely to reflect the social changes discussed earlier. With domestic responsibilities becoming less onerous – and also part-time work becoming more widely available – it is not surprising that many women have sought value and a contribution outside the home. It is also not surprising that the participation in the labour force of mothers in couples is higher than that of single parents (Figure 2.2), since even somewhat limited sharing of domestic tasks is possible for couples.

The corollary is that there is the potential for a growing gulf between work-rich and work-poor households. However, this should be put in context. The British Household Panel Survey in 1991 showed that 15 per cent of households of working age had no earners (Dex and Taylor, 1994). Over half of these had no children or were single-person households. Though this percentage may be unacceptably high, it should also be remembered that in 1991 the unemployment rate was itself 8 per cent. Some of this is the result of the operation of the benefits system (see Social Justice Commission, 1994, for some details). The evidence suggests that if the full-time partner becomes unemployed, it is not worth the other partner continuing in employment. Some of it is the result of the changing distribution of employment opportunities, to which we will return below.

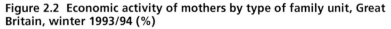

Figure 2.2 Economic activity of mothers by type of family unit, Great Britain, winter 1993/94 (%)

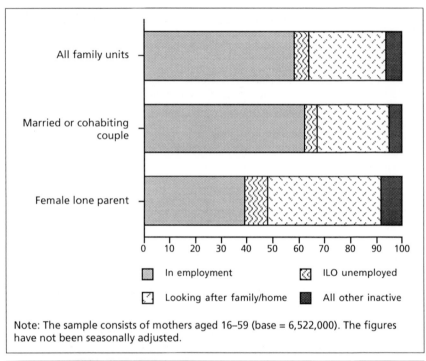

Note: The sample consists of mothers aged 16–59 (base = 6,522,000). The figures have not been seasonally adjusted.

Source: Employment Gazette, *November 1994*

The distribution of earned income between family types has remained fairly constant over the decade. The average earnings of households with the eldest child between 5 and 15 are slightly higher than those of couples with the eldest child under 5, and both are well above other sorts of married couples, lone parents and single persons (Figures 2.3 and 2.4). This suggests that earnings patterns may partly reflect need. Children are expensive and older children more so. Only other households, which include those with more than one adult working but not married, have similar levels of income. This might suggest that the rise of two-earner households is itself a reflection of economic necessity. It does not appear to have generated any kind of increasing gap between households of different types.

Figure 2.3 Average earned income by household type, 1981 (£000s)

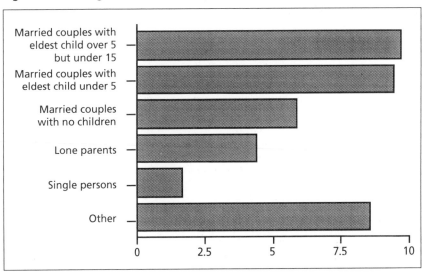

Source: BSL

Figure 2.4 Average earned income by household type, 1991 (£000s)

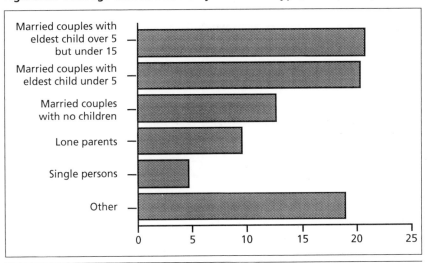

Source: BSL

This seems to suggest that it is to employment opportunities that we must look to analyse any further the sources of poverty in households with earned income.

Employment

Industries

Two fundamental changes to employment patterns have become apparent in the UK over the past decade, though both are expected to moderate in the next ten years. One is the shift away from manufacturing. Although manufacturing output has been growing, this has not resulted in much job creation. Over the decade to 1994, all the manufacturing and production sectors lost jobs – with engineering, the largest of them, losing more than 500,000 (Figure 2.5). But it is in engineering and other manufacturing sectors that the paradigmatic worker of the post-war consensus was to be found: male, working with his hands, semi-

Figure 2.5 Employment changes in the UK (000s)

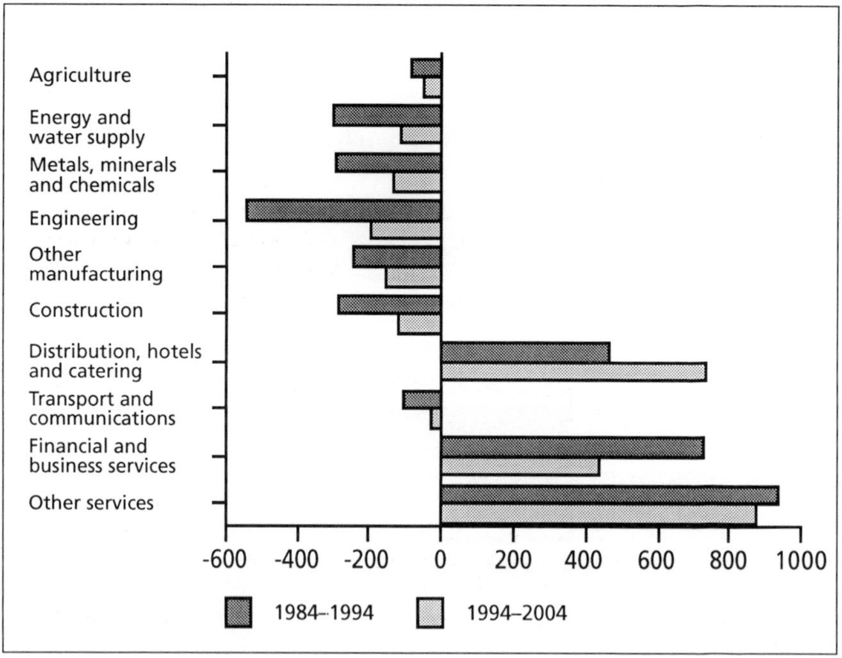

Source: BSL Forecasts

killed. These were the jobs that were created in the light engineering plants, the car factories and the defence engineering and aerospace industries. Some had higher skill levels than others, but also relied on large amounts of production labour. In the 1970s, it was an increasing problem that workers could earn more at semi-skilled production jobs than at skilled ones.

Many, if not most of these jobs, have disappeared along with the factories that produced them. Manufacturing estates are now retail parks or at best business parks, providing jobs for sales assistants, clerical workers and management.

This too is apparent in the figures. The industries that created jobs in the last decade were distribution, financial and business services, and services such as government, health, education and leisure. Some of this change is the result of contracting out: the replacement of the company canteen by a service provided by a catering company; the replacement of an in-house marketing team with the services of consultants.

But it is also the result of a more basic shift mirrored in changes in land use up and down the country. The foundries of Walsall are now the Merry Hill out-of-town retail centre; the car plants of Oxford are becoming a business park; the steel works in Sheffield are now also a major out-of-town shopping centre. The list goes on.

To some extent these changes are set to continue. Manufacturing industry in the UK can be highly successful, but it will not be on the basis of large-scale plants. High-technology units employ much technology but few people. The revival of motor manufacturing on the back of the Japanese companies has turned round the balance of trade in cars, but the industry employs far fewer people than in the 1960s. Robots take the strain.

However, the forecast does suggest that employment losses will be smaller than in the past decade. Greater success in the manufacturing sector and an end to major restructuring will make it possible to slow down job loss. A different pattern may emerge in the erstwhile engines of job creation – services. In particular, as we suggested above, restructuring is likely to hit the service sector. Technical change, more intense competition and possibly greater consumer sophistication are conspiring to make companies in this sector look carefully at cost structures. The impact of privatisation is one part of this pattern: while widening the income differentials within the companies, it has also 'downsized' the workforce.

The financial and business services sector, particularly the former, is also likely to be hard hit. Technical change has made possible the automation of many clerical back-office processes of data entry and paper management, while management of these processes has also been simplified.

Gender

The outcome of this industrial change has been an enormous change in employment by gender. However, the automation of back offices is one example where women's jobs are likely to be lost, as much of the clerical side of data management was done by women.

Figure 2.6 Total employment in the UK

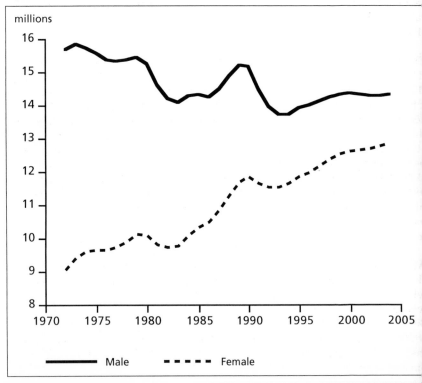

Source: Department of Employment

Even so, it is the service sector and particularly the personal services industries which are likely to be creating jobs, though on a lesser scale. This still means that there will be a continued shift away from the old-style traditional jobs towards those more likely to be part-time and those traditionally done by women. If the trend in the employment by gender for each industry persists, then by 2004 the gap between the number of men and women employed will almost have closed, from seven million in 1972 to less than two million by 2004 (Figure 2.6). However, the rather different sectoral pattern does imply that male employment will have stabilised and even risen again.

In this context, it is worth noting that after considerable concern in recent years that the only jobs being created were part-time ones taken by women, male full-time jobs have started to appear and in 1994 there were also rises in manufacturing employment. Moreover, it should be remembered that not all women take part-time jobs and the number of full-time jobs has also been growing (Figure 2.7).

There is also a continued shift in the occupational mix of employment. Not only do we see the continued decline in manufacturing occupations, but also a rise in the managerial and professional categories. It is the semi-skilled and unskilled jobs that are disappearing fastest. Nickell and Bell (1995) estimate that 20 per cent of the long-run rise in unemployment in Britain in the 1960s and 1970s was due to a fall in the relative demand for unskilled workers. This, of course, may still cover up deskilling within other occupational labels. White-collar jobs have been thought of as requiring a higher level of education but may not be very skilled. Those skilled craft jobs that remain may have become more highly technical as well – especially requiring the acquisition of computer skills. This is probably also true of clerical work, where secretaries are far less likely to do the basic typing, but will need to know how to lay out a document and operate the more sophisticated end of the word-processing package.

At the other end of the spectrum, some professional jobs may be becoming less skilled. The bank manager's scope to exercise his or her own judgement about whether to offer a loan may now be circumscribed by a questionnaire, from whose answers a computer system will decide whether the loan can be offered. Banks are increasingly trying to develop these 'expert systems', where the computer system can replicate the best advice of the best experts. To the extent these are introduced, there will be less skill attached to the jobs of those who operate them.

Whatever the skill content and how it is changing, there is a well-established

Figure 2.7 Female employment in the UK

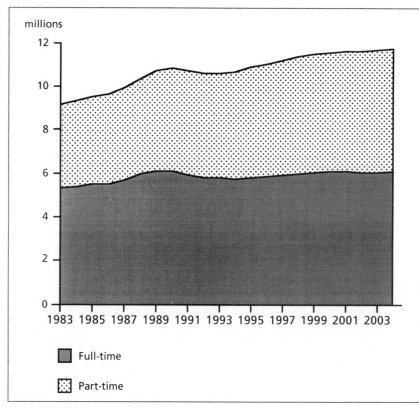

Source: Department of Employment

trend towards more jobs labelled managerial and professional. This is also partly because one of the areas of expected growth is in business and personal services, which will require doctors, health professionals, teachers, lawyers, accountants, etc. The professions and managerial positions have been biased towards men in the past. This is likely to be less the case in the future. Health care and teaching have, of course, been a traditional source of women's employment, but recently, for example, more women than men have been becoming solicitors. The glass ceiling may be in place at the top of the professional ladder, but in terms of sheer numbers the scope for changing the balance is clear.

This is likely to be exacerbated by women's apparent greater success in school in recent years. While girls' better performance in education tended to tail off at puberty in the past, this is no longer the case.

Flexibility

This is a much overused and imprecise term. It can be taken to mean the ability of the employer to hire and fire – to have flexible numbers in the workforce. It can mean the ability to change wage rates quickly and easily. It can mean that the employer can provide flexible working hours to meet employees' needs, and flexible career paths with multi-skilling. It can also mean the flexibility of individuals to pursue different careers at different times in their lives and to acquire different skills as they do so. The implications of these different kinds of flexibility for poverty, opportunity and security are very different.

The same is true to some extent of temporary work. If you want a secure job with an open-ended commitment, then temporary work is undesirable. If the availability of temporary work fills a need for something now which you do not expect to last for ever, then it may be highly desirable. Where the balance should be struck is not obvious. If the provision of secure jobs jeopardises the existence of all the jobs in the long run, then again the balance is not clear.

Having said this, there are aspects of flexibility that could have an impact on reducing opportunity and increasing insecurity. One is the rise in temporary employment. Though this is a well-publicised phenomenon, it is not clear that it is really very widespread. It is perhaps the extension of such contracts into the areas where media comment is made, and into professional activities that have always seen themselves as quintessentially secure, that has made this change more apparent than real. Labour Force Survey data shows that 6.5 per cent of employees and self-employed persons were in seasonal, temporary or casual work or on fixed contracts in 1994. This is up from 5.3 per cent a decade earlier. However, it is worth noting that seasonal jobs have remained fairly stable, while the proportion on fixed contracts has doubled. Even so, this is from 1.5 per cent to only 3.5 per cent (Beatson, 1995).

Another possibility is that flexibility means that there are more people on low pay, or on low pay for a greater proportion of their working lives. It is to this that we now turn.

Earnings

Low pay

There is no doubt that the income distribution has widened. To some extent, as the Rowntree Commission has shown (Hills, 1995), this is the result of benefits not keeping up with incomes, combined with a rise of people on benefit incomes: in other words, less access to work opportunities for some groups.

It is also the result of a widening income distribution even for those in work. By 1993, the proportion of the median wage earned by males in full-time employment in the bottom decile was 62.7 per cent – down from 69.4 per cent in 1978. This proportion was one that had been stable since records were first collected in the late 1880s (Hills, 1995). Low pay levels can also be associated with higher employment levels for women compared to men. The average pay

Figure 2.8 Women's hourly pay as a percentage of men's; employees on adult rates, excluding overtime

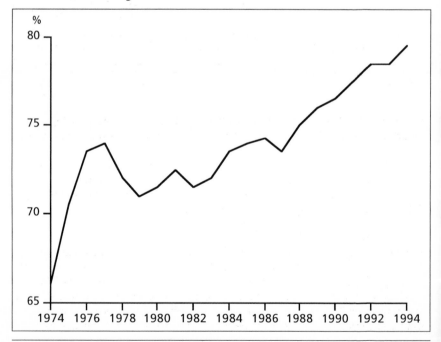

Source: Employment Gazette, *December 1994*

Figure 2.9 Earned income as a percentage of total income

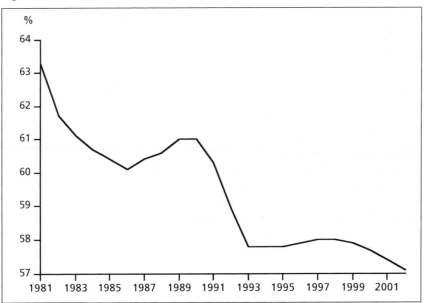

Source: BSL

for women is well below that for men, although it has been steadily rising (Figure 2.8). Nonetheless, women's earnings are only 80 per cent those of men.

Lack of skill is an important determinant: with a strong correlation between a lack of education and non-participation in the labour market and with low incomes (Glyn, 1995). In the UK there has been a fall of one-quarter in the relative incomes from employment of the least qualified.

Earned income
Another important phenomenon is the rising importance of non-earned income, which is expected to go on increasing. At the beginning of the 1980s, 63 per cent of household income was earned. By 1993, this proportion was down to 57 per cent (Figure 2.9). The reasons for the fall are partly due to falling participation in the labour market; they are also due to the increasing importance of benefit income. The interaction between benefits and pay is therefore important to poverty and is investigated elsewhere in this volume.

Conclusion

There are no simple answers to the conundrum of where work is going to come from. The conclusions here therefore remain partial and indeed will require further investigation if there are to be any real answers. The first conclusion concerns participation. We have seen that one reason for rising unemployment might well be the increasing desire to be in the workforce, at least for prime age groups. It is still unclear whether this is likely to stabilise. In part it also depends on the widely held view that work is the way one's contribution to society and the community is measured. Whether this should continue to be the case is something investigated elsewhere.

There is little likelihood, however, of a rapid change in attitudes. A willingness to work in other ways also depends on such forms being able to add value for the individual. Voluntary work may be an alternative to paid work in terms of its use of time, but is no real choice if money income is required to pay for shelter, food and the other necessities of life.

It is likely that pressure for jobs will increase rather than fall. Changes in the structure of the workforce will probably result in demand for more flexible career paths, however. A higher proportion of women workers may well mean more demand for flexible hours, part-time work and even temporary contracts.

At the same time there seems to be some evidence that the structure of labour demand from employers is changing. In part, this may well reflect changes in supply patterns. Disentangling these can of course be extremely difficult, not to say impossible. Some conclusions can be drawn from the changes in product demand. The continued shift to service sector employment, and even within manufacturing away from traditional production lines, will put a premium on clerical and computer skills and on literacy and numeracy. The pressure for higher levels of education is almost certain to increase.

The ability to provide settled jobs for standard shifts is also likely to change as companies need to become more responsive to demand shifts. This is also likely to be the result of more contracting out and specialised service provision between businesses.

None of this necessarily means that fewer jobs are available, though it does mean that the low skilled and those unwilling to change their labour provision will find it increasingly difficult. These changes also mean that there will be more frequent job changes. Currently about 12–15 per cent of people change their economic status each year (Beatson, 1995). More frequent spells of unemployment are one possible consequence, and so too are lower lifetime earnings, if experience is a determinant of earnings.

The role of experience in any one job may become less important. Equally, this possible change will start to reverse a trend that has been apparent over a long while: the importance of internal labour markets. The role of internal labour markets has been analysed over a long period to explain observed differentials that did not appear to reflect any other market patterns. It may be that these will become less important.

All of this suggests that the division between work-rich and work-poor households may intensify. The unskilled will have a hard time and so too will those with more traditionally oriented skills. It seems likely that the households with one member with higher skills will have other skilled members too.

One mitigating factor may be the extension of flexibility in its career sense. The greater ability not to work and still have access to a career path, if it comes about, may spread work more widely, at least across the more skilled portions of the workforce. Even so, this will still leave an open question about income distribution. If it is the case that work becomes more concentrated into particular portions of people's lives, it leaves open how they are to be supported or will support themselves in the remaining period. In part this is a question about the levels of taxation and benefits. There is already pressure to reduce the benefit bill – both for income support and pensions. If people are to be able to support themselves in their non-working periods, this means that financial institutions will need to be much more flexible than they are now about how loans are made and what constitutes security for loans.

References

Beatson, M. (1995) *Labour Market Flexibility*, Employment Department Research Paper no. 48

Brannen, J., Meszaros, G., Moss, P. and Poland, G. (1994) *Employment and Family Life, A Review of Research in the UK*, Employment Department Research Paper no. 41

Dex, S. and Taylor, M. (1994) 'Household employment in 1991', *Employment Gazette*, October

Dex, S., Clark, A. and Taylor, M. (1995) *Household Labour Supply*, Employment Department Research Paper no. 43

Employment Gazette (1988) 'Labour force outlook to 1995', March

Employment Gazette (1995) 'British labour force projections, 1995–2006', April

Glyn, A. (1995) 'Unemployment and inequality', *Oxford Review of Economic Policy*, vol. 11, no.1

Hills, J. (1995) *Joseph Rowntree Foundation Inquiry into Income and Wealth*, vol. 2, Joseph Rowntree Foundation

Nickell, S. and Bell, B. (1995) 'The collapse in demand for the unskilled and unemployment across the OECD', *Oxford Review of Economic Policy*, vol. 11, no.1

Social Justice Commission (1994) *Social Justice, Strategies for National Renewal*, Vintage

3 The place of part-time employment

Patricia Hewitt

Workforce trends

Two substantial and related trends – the growth in women's employment and the growth in part-time working – have helped to transform the labour market in this country over the last 30 years. In 1971, nearly two-thirds of the workforce were men. By the end of 1994, almost half of all employees were women. In some regions of the country they were already in the majority, although men remain the majority of the growing numbers of self-employed everywhere. Nearly half of those women employees were working part-time, as were some one in ten of employed men. Although employers have often attributed the increase in part-time jobs to the needs of women employees, other forces – independent of women's employment – are driving production systems towards a growing reliance upon non-standard employment. Thus, part-time employment, most of which continues to be taken by women, needs to be seen as part of a larger change in the labour market as the United Kingdom and other EU countries move from an industrial to a 'post-industrial' economy.

The extent and distribution of part-time employment have been summarised in Chapter 2. This chapter starts by analysing the reasons, on both the supply and the demand sides, for the growth of part-time and, more generally, 'flexible' employment. It then considers whether such employment should be promoted or discouraged by public policy. Finally, it considers what policy changes are required in labour market regulation, social security and child-care policy, if flexible employment is to fulfil its potential to meet the needs of a growing number of women and men.

Working patterns

By way of a preliminary observation, however, it is important to understand the extraordinary variety of working patterns to be found within the British economy. 'Part-time' employment includes the clerical worker on a regular, 24-hour-a-week contract; the DIY sales operator working a 3-day 'weekend' for full-time wages; the local authority job-sharer on 17 hours per week with membership of a pension scheme; the shop assistant whose hours vary each week; the cleaner who works for 3 hours per week, and the production-line operator on a zero hours contract. Add to those the full-time employees who regularly work evenings, nights, Saturdays and/or Sundays, and it is easy to see why only one in three of British employees works what is still often regarded as a 'normal' week – 9 to 5, Mondays to Fridays (Marsh, 1991).

There is also some evidence of an increase in very-short-hours working since the end of the 1980s. The average weekly hours worked by part-time employees fell from 19 in 1979 to 17.6 in 1994 (Butcher and Hart, 1995). Analysis of the Labour Force Survey 1993 suggested that in the 12 months to December 1993, the numbers working below 8 hours per week rose by 150,000 – an increase of twice the rate of those working between 16 and 30 hours per week, and three times the rate of those working between 8 and 15 hours (Bassett, 1994). On the other hand, comparing the bottom of this recession with the bottom of the last, average part-time hours in 1993 (17.4) were actually higher than in 1984 (16.9) (Butcher and Hart, 1995).[1] A large proportion of jobs offering very short hours, however, appear to be taken by students who are unlikely to be available for longer hours of work.

The increase in employment among women – specifically women with intermediate or higher educational qualifications – is common to all industrialised countries. In the UK and some other industrialised countries, however, nearly all the increase in employment has taken the form of part-time work. The fact that women continue to take prime responsibility for the care of children is clearly one element in the picture. Since, however, it is a factor common to all industrial countries, it cannot of itself explain why part-time employment varies so substantially between, say, France or Germany and the United Kingdom. To account for the British situation, we need instead to look at the interaction between women's family responsibilities, changes in the production system, the nature of labour market regulation, the tax and social security system, and attitudes towards the care of dependants.

As we saw in Chapter 2, the new jobs now being created in the United Kingdom – including part-time jobs – are overwhelmingly to be found within the rapidly expanding service sector. Rising real incomes and (until the mid-1980s) falling working hours for those in full-time employment have increased demand for leisure services. The growth in employment among women has increased the demand for services that substitute for domestic labour and also for services outside normal office hours. The marked drop in Christian worship has changed people's expectations of Sunday activities, one result of which has been a sharp increase in Sunday trading and, in consequence, a change in the law. The increase in the number of very elderly people, coupled with the reduction in the number of women available to work as volunteers or to care for relatives full-time, has increased demand for professional domiciliary services during weekends and evenings and also weekdays. The '24-hour service economy' may be an exaggeration, but extended opening hours are increasingly common. Some enterprises – not only the emergency services – do operate round the clock and round the year, while others face extraordinary variations in demand at different times of the day, week or season of the year.

An efficient service sector cannot operate, however, based solely on traditional, full-time, year-round working patterns. Instead, employers seeking to extend and/or vary their operating hours to meet changing demand – while simultaneously trying to hold down labour costs and prices – have increasingly turned to part-time and other forms of 'flexible' employment. As one senior manager in a large retail department store expressed it: 'If "full-time" is the hours the store opens, then no-one here works full-time. After all, the store is open six days a week, 9 to 6 three days, 9 to 8 two days and 9 to 5 on Saturdays. All of us are part-time, compared to that.'

Competitive pressures are, similarly, forcing manufacturing industry to review its traditional shift systems, with many companies seeking to extend plant operating hours to raise the return on high-tech capital equipment, and others requiring seasonal variation in their labour force to meet fluctuations in demand. Pressure for shorter working hours, notably from the German and British engineering unions, has encouraged enterprises to decouple factory operating hours from individual working hours, reorganising shift patterns across periods of a fortnight, month or six months, achieving productivity gains by eliminating 'downtime' and reducing overtime payments, and simultaneously cutting individuals' average working hours.

Thus, competitive pressures and structural changes within both a shrinking manufacturing and a growing service sector are driving an increase in part-time and other forms of non-standard employment. The desire of employers for greater flexibility does not differ greatly across the European Union. What does differ, however, and helps to explain why the change is so much more marked in the UK, is the nature of labour market and trading-hours regulation. In every other EU country, standard weekly working hours are set by law (or, in Denmark, by nationwide collective agreements). In the UK, by contrast, there is no tradition of universal working-hours regulation. The protective legislation, mainly dating from the last century, which limited working hours for certain industries (such as mining and bakeries), as well as for women and young people in manual trades, was largely abolished in the 1980s. Similarly, the restrictions to be found in other EU countries on the use of temporary and subcontract labour do not exist in Britain, and minimum-wage legislation, never universal nor particularly generous, has now disappeared altogether. Working hours are considerably more varied here than in other EU countries.

Regulatory framework

At one end of a spectrum, therefore, we have a country like Germany where regulatory restrictions on shop opening and individual working hours combine with high minimum wages to block off the development of personal services in the private sector; where the maintenance of a high level of male industrial employment at high wages makes it possible for one male worker to support a family; and where a restricted public service sector (notably, a school day traditionally ending at lunchtime in the Western *Länder* and the closure of the child-care centres in the Eastern *Länder*) makes it very difficult in any case for women with children to remain in employment. At the other end of the spectrum we have the United Kingdom, where the withdrawal in the 1980s of earlier regulation has helped to encourage the growth of a service sector offering a wide variety of working hours and conditions, particularly in stereotypically female occupations, and where the decline of male industrial employment is an important element in explaining the decline in single-earner families.

Besides the changing nature of production and the influence of the regulatory system, however, we also need to consider the impact on both employers and employees of the tax and benefits system. In Germany and most other EU countries, minimum wages, working conditions and social security contributions apply regardless of hours; in the UK, where no 'equal treatment' principle applies, both employment legislation and the structure of national insurance contributions create important incentives towards part-time employment. Until a House of Lords ruling in 1994, employers knew that by keeping normal weekly working hours below 16, they would be exempt from the laws on unfair dismissal and redundancy in respect of an employee with less than 5 years' continuous service; employment for less than 8 hours per week, for however long a period, could never qualify for statutory protection. Despite these provisions, at the end of the 1970s 60 per cent of women part-time employees qualified for employment protection – nearly the same proportion of women full-timers (67 per cent). By 1989, however, the proportion of part-time employees who qualified had fallen to below 50 per cent – reflecting not only the mid-1980s growth in part-time working (many of the new employees not yet having achieved the necessary two or five years' continuous employment) but also a decline in the hours generally worked by part-time employees (Hakim, 1989; Marsh, 1991).

It is not clear how far employment legislation accounts for the growth in part-time employment of below 16 hours per week. As Catherine Hakim pointed out in her analysis of the 1986 Labour Force Survey, the peaks in employment at around 10 and 15 hours were more likely to be multiples of 5 days per week than attempts to avoid the law (Hakim, 1989). In any case, European Union legislation, as applied by the House of Lords, will reduce whatever incentive employers previously had to avoid employment protection. The recent growth in jobs offering very short hours may, however, reflect the structure of national insurance contributions, where employees earning below the Lower Earnings Limit (currently £57 per week) pay nothing, while employers' contributions (zero for earnings below this threshold) start at 3.6 per cent on earnings between £57 and £100, rising in two further stages to 10.2 per cent on earnings above £200 per week. Employers who can organise their labour requirements as a series of short part-time jobs will pay substantially less in contributions than if they employ an equivalent number of full-time employees.

The point is vividly illustrated by the employer discovered by the Low Pay Network in Stirling to be advertising 91 part-time jobs, only four of which paid more than £56 a week. If the same hours had been worked by 28 full-time employees, the Treasury would have gained over £40,000 in tax and contributions. Whatever the relative weights of different explanatory factors, evidently employment protection legislation, national insurance contributions and the changing demands of the service sector have all been working together to promote part-time rather than full-time employment.

Child care

The final factor to be considered is social attitudes towards the care of dependants. The practical and emotional care of children remains primarily women's responsibility. Although time use surveys in this and other countries confirm that men are spending an increasing amount of time in both routine housework and the care of children, the time devoted by women to children remains substantially higher. A growing proportion of the public, particularly among younger respondents, believes that housework and child care should be shared equally between women and men; the reality, however, remains very different.[2] For men, the time available for family and leisure is that left over from employment; for many women with children or elderly dependants, the time available for employment and leisure is that left over from family.

The pros and cons of part-time working

The disadvantages of part-time employment are substantial. As an Equal Opportunities Commission survey of working hours confirmed, part-time employment is concentrated in the service sector, particularly public services, and is more common among manual than non-manual employees (Marsh, 1991). In white-collar occupations, part-time work tends to involve the less well-paid and lower-status clerical and secretarial jobs. In manual occupations, part-time employees form a majority of cleaners, counter-hands, shelf assistants and other routine jobs. On average, part-time employees earn less per hour than full-time workers; they are also less likely to qualify for membership of a pension scheme, or to receive training or promotion. As we have seen, part-time employees working less than 16 hours per week are discriminated against in statutory employment law.

From the individual's point of view, the convenience offered by less than full-time hours is often achieved at the price of slipping down the occupational ladder. Since most part-time workers are women, the extension of part-time employment may, in practice, deepen gender segregation in employment. Full-time, well-rewarded career occupations may be reserved for men and women willing to sacrifice time with their family, while women (and a few men) who want a different balance between work and family are confined to a 'mummy track' without career prospects.

Since part-time employment almost never pays enough to support a family (and perhaps not even a single person), part-time jobs can only be taken by those with another earner in the family – often, in practice, women married to men in employment. For this group, the tax and benefits system offers substantial incentives to work part-time, with no deduction at all from earnings below the national insurance contribution threshold. For women whose partners are unemployed or earning a low wage topped up by family credit, benefit withdrawal starts at a much lower point, creating effective disincentives for the woman to take work.

Thus, it is argued, the rise in part-time working is helping to create a gulf between 'work-rich' families, with more than one job, and 'work-poor' families with no job at all, while offering little or nothing to most of the unemployed who need a full-time wage. Instead, the unemployed and the insecurely employed face the prospect of patching together different part-time jobs to obtain a living wage, without any job offering much in the way of prospects of security. Some support for this fear is offered by the steady increase in the number of people holding second jobs, from 380,000 in 1979 to 1.13 million in 1994 (Butcher and Hart, 1995). And as we have already seen, from a macro-economic viewpoint, part-time employment may seriously undermine the tax base.

Should Government therefore try to reverse the apparently inexorable rise in part-time employment? Quite apart from the practical difficulties of such an approach, we need to consider alongside the disadvantages the very real advantages of part-time working.

First, despite lower pay and poorer conditions, part-time employees routinely express themselves as more satisfied with their working hours, their jobs and the time they have available for themselves and their families. Of course, it is possible that part-time employees are more satisfied with their working conditions simply because family responsibilities leave them with no real choice. In my own qualitative research, however, I found that most mothers with part-time jobs were clear that they had made a positive choice to work less than full-time hours and would not have changed their working pattern even if full-time substitute child care had been available. That conclusion was borne out by the 1990 British Social Attitudes Survey, which asked mothers in employment to imagine they could choose whatever child-care arrangements they liked. Even when faced with the possibilities of a workplace nursery, a free child-care nursery or a childminder at home, over half of these women – and two-thirds of those with school-age children – said that they would prefer to work only while the children were at school. Just as popular, particularly for children aged under five, was having a relative (including the child's father) care for them at least some of the time while the mother was working (Witherspoon and Prior, 1991).

Only a minority of part-time employees – including part-time male employees – say that they would prefer to work full-time.[3] Nonetheless, there is a real mismatch between mothers' preferences and the reality: about one in four of the women who want to stay at home after having a baby ends up in employment, while the same proportion of those who do stay at home would prefer to be in a job (McRae, 1993).

There is also evidence that a significant proportion of full-time employees – including, not surprisingly, a higher proportion of people over 50 – would prefer to work part-time at some stage in their lives. According to an NOP poll commissioned by the TUC (1995), over 70 per cent of those working over 40 hours want to work less; 53 per cent of women would prefer to work part-time (only 40 per cent were in fact doing so), as would 14 per cent of men (only 3 per cent were doing so).

As a growing proportion of the workforce confronts the need to update their skills at least once and probably more often during their working lives, the demand will grow for part-time or full-time 'education sabbaticals'. Although less important than family responsibilities or personal ill health, the desire to learn new skills already helps to explain the popularity of schemes which allow full-time employees to reduce their working hours. For instance, the Inland Revenue's pioneering agreement to allow full-time employees with family commitments or other special circumstances to opt for part-time working has benefited more than 10 per cent of its workforce in the last decade. When British Airways decided to 'downsize' by offering employees the option of shorter hours – with the same hourly wage, pension rights and other conditions, enhanced pension rights for the over-50s and a cash bonus – they had no shortage of volunteers. Indeed, management not only met its targets for a smaller workforce, but saved on the cost of redundancy payments as well.

Second, it is important to recognise that many disadvantages associated with part-time work are the result of policies that can be changed. The penalties imposed by employment protection legislation have already largely been removed. A level playing field of employment rights, as proposed below, would tackle the exclusion of part-time employees from pension schemes and training opportunities.

The third point to make in support of an extension of part-time employment is the contribution which it can make towards reducing unemployment. It must be stressed that shorter hours do not, of themselves, offer any cure for unemployment. Reductions in full-time working hours, as the engineering industry for example has found, are often compensated for by increased productivity, so that no increase in employment is required. Nonetheless, particularly for a firm faced with the prospect of redundancies, cuts in working hours can make it possible to avoid adding to the numbers of unemployed. I have referred already to the experience of British Airways. In Germany, Volkswagen – facing a dramatic drop in demand – agreed with the trade union to move to a four-day week. This proved so popular with full-time employees that, when demand recovered and increased production hours were required, many chose to remain on four days. (It must be said, of course, that even a four-day Volkswagen worker earns more than the average German – let alone British – industrial employee.)

Nor should we fall into the 'lump of labour' fallacy, assuming that there is only a limited amount of work to be shared out. Clearly, there is work which needs doing: the issue is how to generate the demand which translates that need into jobs. At the same time, for any given total demand for labour – or any increase in demand for labour over a period – the length of working hours will determine the numbers of people employed. Within the European Union,

ountries with lower average full-time hours and a high proportion of part-time
employees secure employment for a higher proportion of their population than
those with high average full-time hours and fewer part-time workers. The UK
offers both patterns simultaneously. For men, increasingly long hours have gone
with falling levels of employment; for women, a growth in part-time work has
accompanied rising levels of employment. Reversing the growth of non-
employment in this country requires attention to the distribution, as well as the
generation, of employment.

Home and work

My final point is more complex and depends upon the model of equal
opportunities – and, behind that, the model of family policy – which one wants
policy makers and employers to adopt. The full-time employment of men, in
conditions where men are the majority of the workforce, depends upon the
availability of enough women to be mothers and housekeepers for nearly half of
their adult working lifetime. In turn, the availability of women for work in the
home depends upon male employment offering a 'family wage' sufficient to
meet family aspirations – as well as, of course, the willingness of women to
prefer family to paid work. Since most men can no longer earn enough to
support what is regarded as a comfortable (or, in many cases, even adequate)
family lifestyle, and since most women now have clear aspirations for the
independence and social contact that even low-paid employment offers, the
former division of paid and unpaid work can no longer be taken for granted. In
its place, the women's movement of the 1970s implicitly put a new model of
full-time employment for both women and men – with child-care services
required to fill the gap left behind in the home. Much of the present debate
about the need for an extension of nursery education and child care rests upon
the same belief that all parents wish to work full-time and should be enabled to
do so. And at the full-time end of the labour market – where manual workers
are required to work extremely long hours, and managers and professionals
either choose to do so or have little choice if their careers are to prosper –
employers cling to the old assumption that every worker has a wife to take care
of home and family.

But a new model of two full-time breadwinners relying upon substitute care for
children and other dependants will not do. There is ample evidence from the
USA, where part-time employment is comparatively rare, of the loss suffered by
children who see too little of their parents (Etzioni, 1994; Hewlett, 1991).[4] The
costs of good-quality substitute child care are so substantial that, even in the
Scandinavian countries where socialised child care has traditionally been

available, policy makers are increasingly emphasising time off for parents, as well as nurseries for children, as part of a balanced child-care package. As we have seen, mothers in this country express a clear preference that they and, where possible, their partners or other members of the family should look after children themselves, with working hours tailored to fit family needs. And not surprisingly, women with children and full-time jobs – even if many of those jobs are professional and well paid – experience the highest levels of stress and tiredness. Expecting mothers to see as little of their children as fathers have traditionally done will not improve the lives of children, women or men.

The reorganisation of working time is, therefore, central to the creation of a new balance between employment and family – in other words, to the redistribution of paid and unpaid work between women and men. It is also required by a serious commitment to equal opportunities in employment. Women are unlikely to be able to contribute the best of their abilities to the economy if they continue to face the unpalatable choice between competing on men's terms, trying to balance increasingly long working hours with an unequal share of family responsibilities, or trading acceptable working hours for a blocked career. A different approach is required.

Choice

Before turning to policy specifics, it will help to specify the 'end game'. Much of the debate about working hours has stressed the need for a shorter working week. In France, for instance, parties of both left and right have considered a statutory reduction in the working week as a means of reducing unemployment. Such an approach in the UK would make the mistake of ignoring not only our very different regulatory tradition, but also the clear evidence that different people have very different working-time preferences. Contrary to the widespread assumption that a 30-hour, five-day week is the ideal to aim for, women with children tend to prefer longer holidays and/or term-time working. For both men and women, a four-day week is often the most popular choice, even at the expense of longer daily working hours (Hewitt, 1993). In any case, it is only a minority of the population at any one time who have dependent children, and there is no reason to impose upon the rest a pattern of work designed to suit families. Nor do all individuals and households have the same income needs: for the two-parent family with children, maintaining two incomes may be the priority, while the individual or couple whose mortgage is paid off and children grown is in a position to make a different trade-off between time and money. Policy makers – and employers – should make a virtue of the fact that most people want to work different hours at different stages of their lives, and should aim to increase the range of occupations offering a real choice of working-time arrangements.

If the goal, then, is to increase the choice available to individuals over their working hours and, in particular, to meet the widespread demand for shorter hours, we need to consider what an appropriate regulatory framework might be. The British Government has consistently argued that the best regulation is the least, and that the growing variety of working-time arrangements available in the UK is a direct result of labour market deregulation. As I have already indicated, it is certainly true that Britain's (de)regulatory regime has helped to encourage the growth of part-time working, while any attempt to impose a single, standard working week would be quite inappropriate. But deregulation is not an adequate strategy for the future.

First, the counterpart to the growth in short-hours jobs in the UK is the increase in hours for full-time employees, particularly men, to the point where average male full-time working hours are now among the longest in Europe (Marsh, 1991). Many of the employees working on average 45–50 hours or more per week have no choice at all in the matter and, under present legislation, little protection against employers' excessive demands. At the other end of the working-hours spectrum, deregulation has left individuals vulnerable to the imposition of 'zero hours' contracts which enable the employer to shift all the risks of fluctuating demand to the employee. If there is no work available, the 'employee' receives nothing; being required to be on call, however, makes it impossible to seek other employment and may result in disqualification from benefits.

The second problem is that very long working hours may be damaging to the health and safety of both employees and those whom they serve. The risks associated with the extremely long hours worked by junior hospital doctors are now seen to be unacceptable. In a very different sector, the official enquiry into the Clapham Junction railway disaster in December 1988, which killed 35 people, found that the senior technician responsible for the faulty wiring that caused the accident had been working a 7-day week for the previous 13 weeks (Hidden, 1989).

Third, it is important to stress that the 'free market' in working hours which the Government claims to have created is not neutral between different working-hours arrangements. As we have seen, both employment legislation and the national insurance system create artificial incentives to employers and, in the latter case, employees, to hold down hours of work regardless of the needs of the enterprise or individual. Furthermore, the social security system creates barriers between unemployed people and the part-time jobs which form a growing proportion of generally available vacancies. More appropriate labour market regulation, coupled with reform of the social security system, is required to extend the benefits of working-time flexibility while reducing, as far as possible, the disadvantages of the present situation.

As well as discouraging or outlawing undesirable practices, regulation can play a positive role in promoting choice. 'Passive' labour market regulation allowed for the spread of part-time working, usually (although not always) in response to the needs of enterprises and employees. 'Active' regulation, on the other hand, was required to make paid maternity leave available beyond a few best-practice companies. Similarly, a modernised regulatory regime could help to spread new opportunities, such as educational sabbaticals or voluntary reductions in working time.

In the final section of this chapter, therefore, I look at the three policy areas in which action is required: labour market regulation; the social security and tax system; and the provision of services, including child care.

Labour market regulation

As working patterns become more varied, the distinctions drawn by British employment law become increasingly difficult to justify. The problem of trying to find an adequate definition of 'full-time' work is underlined by the fact that, whereas employment law draws the line at 16 hours – contrary to employment statistics which use 30 hours as the norm – the social security system has fluctuated between 16 and 25 hours per week to distinguish between 'out-of-work' and 'in-work' benefits. The House of Lords has already held that a part-time employee working between 8 and 16 hours per week should qualify for redundancy pay and unfair dismissal on the same basis as someone working over 16 hours. That ruling should be reflected in statute, by adopting the European Commission proposal that employment rights should apply to all employees working on average at least 8 hours per week. With a level playing field of employment rights, employees would know that they would receive the same legal protection whatever their hours or pattern of work, while employers would be free to organise working hours without facing artificial incentives to hold down working hours. (It can certainly be argued that even employees working fewer than 8 hours in one job should be protected too, particularly since they may be combining several different jobs in order to earn a living. Given the existing pressures on industrial tribunals, however, and the administrative problems facing employers, an 8-hours threshold seems a reasonable compromise. If the growth in very-short-hours working continues, it might be necessary to review this question, at least in respect of multiple job holders.)

This 'equal treatment' principle should also extend to other terms and conditions, including hourly rates of pay and membership of an occupational pension scheme. Again, the intention would be to create a level playing field, removing artificial incentives to employers to favour part-time over full-time employees. Some, including the present Government, argue that an increase in part-time employment rights, by increasing the costs to employers, would inhibit the growth in part-time employment. Although some such effect might be apparent, for most employers the pressures for more flexible working patterns are unlikely to be outweighed by a change in the legal position.

A level playing field on working hours need not imply, however, complete neutrality towards all working-time arrangements. As I argued earlier, some practices impose unacceptable risks on individual employees and even on members of the public. Furthermore, if Government wishes to promote a better balance between employment and family life, then it needs to tackle the problem posed by employers whose organisational culture values extremely long working hours, to the detriment of family and personal life. A level playing field, in other words, requires a boundary fence.

Appropriate boundaries could be created by implementing the European Directive on Working Time. Although the Directive has been accepted in principle by the British Government, an opt-out has been negotiated which delays full implementation for ten years and requires bureaucratic procedures for listing 'volunteers' for overtime. The Directive, which sets the objective of a 48-hour maximum working week and a 13-hour maximum working day, contains many exceptions for particular industries, circumstances and occupations. Nonetheless, it requires proper protection for health and safety for those who have no choice about working long hours or shifts. Its acceptance would also symbolise and help to publicise the need to reduce very long working hours. 'Zero hours' contracts should also be outlawed. With those exceptions, however, there should be no restrictions on working-time flexibility.

By definition, flexibility cannot be imposed. Regulation could be used, however, to increase opportunities for flexibility. For example, following the British Airways practice, redundancy legislation could be amended to require employers contemplating redundancies to start by offering voluntary reductions in working hours. Without attempting to impose unrealistic limits on working hours, this move would also help to signal the need to reduce the working hours of full-timers, rather than relying on fewer people to work even longer hours. Far from imposing extra costs on employers, the policy would save employers the cost of redundancy payments.

The introduction of statutory maternity leave was a recognition of the need to modify full-time, continuous employment patterns to take account of family responsibilities. Following practice in Scandinavian and some other European countries, the next stage would be to make up to 12 months' unpaid parental leave available to either the father or the mother, on a full-time or part-time basis. Since it would clearly be unrealistic in the present economic climate to require employers to offer paid leave for this period, the new right would effectively be an extension of the existing right to reinstatement. A reformed national insurance system could offer some parental leave benefit, while employers should be encouraged to negotiate more generous arrangements. Although the absence of payment would reduce the numbers who could take advantage of the new entitlement, even unpaid leave would help to ensure that those parents who are enabled by a partner's income or their own savings to stop work and care for a young child could return to employment at the appropriate level.

A similar opportunity to move from paid employment to unpaid family work could be created with the establishment of 'carers' leave' along the same lines as maternity and parental leave, to help meet the needs of those now forced to curtail employment in order to care for dependent relatives. In the USA, the Family and Medical Leave Act 1993 established a statutory right to 12 weeks' unpaid, job-protected leave for people with family needs, including the care of an elderly relative – although only firms employing more than 50 people are covered.

Finally, a new entitlement to a 'learning sabbatical' would simultaneously promote working-time flexibility and help to raise human capital investment. This could take the form of the 'Baker days' recently proposed by Harriet Harman MP, which would give employees a right to perhaps five days' education and training a year. Alternatively, educational leave could be available for accumulation over a longer period. As with parental leave, rights to *payment* from employers may not be feasible; again, a reformed national insurance fund should offer some payment.

The tax and benefits systems

The fact that most part-time employees are women married to men with full-time jobs reflects, in part, the growing dependence of unemployed and low-paid men on means-tested benefits. Those benefits, because they depend on a test of household means, inevitably create disincentives to the woman considering employment. The redistribution of employment that is required in the British labour market will, therefore, require a reversal of the present policy of favouring means-tested over insurance-based benefits. National insurance benefits have the virtue of providing individual benefits in return for individual contributions, creating an incentive to an unemployed person's partner to remain in or take up employment. The jobseeker's allowance, by halving the duration of unemployment insurance benefit, will instead reduce work incentives for the partners of unemployed men.

Rather than extending means-tested benefits further, we need a modernised social insurance system, making it easier – not harder – for people who lose their job to claim unemployment insurance (Commission on Social Justice, 1994; Field, 1995). National insurance should therefore be reformed to reflect the needs of part-time and occasional as well as full-time, full-year workers. The calculation of contributions for benefit entitlements should be made over a longer period, and with fewer obstacles, than now. The 'availability for work' rules should be reformed to recognise that some people only wish to be available for part-time work (and, conversely, should not treat people seeking full-time work as only available for part-time employment once they have, by default, accepted a short-lived, part-time job). Unemployment and other benefits should be available on a part-time basis, to meet the needs of both the willing part-time worker who has become unemployed and the unwilling part-time worker who continues to look for a full-time (or second part-time) job.[5]

Although lone parents in this country are significantly less likely to be in employment than other mothers, they are more likely when they work to do so full-time, since the gain from part-time work is minimal once benefit withdrawals take effect. Special efforts are required to encourage lone parents to take up part-time employment, where that suits their family responsibilities better than full-time work, by allowing them to combine part-time earnings with benefits (and maintenance, where that is available). Ironically, because family credit was designed for a single-earner household, it creates none of the disincentive effects for lone parents that it creates in two-parent families. A higher earnings disregard for income support claimants, coupled with a maintenance disregard, would encourage more lone parents to take up employment for less than 16 hours per week (the threshold for family credit), while a lower withdrawal rate for housing benefit would help to reduce the 'poverty plateau' suffered by all recipients of means-tested benefits.

The national insurance system should also be reformed to enable people to spread income from periods in employment – which, for men, are substantially shorter than for previous generations – to periods out of employment (which, for both men and women, are being increased as life expectancy increases). As Frank Field and I have both recently argued, this will best be achieved by restoring the actuarial element of national insurance that Beveridge originally intended, rather than hoping to achieve the very substantial transfers of income required through continued reliance on a pay-as-you-go system. Following the model of pensions, where a proportion of most employees' national insurance contributions (NICs) is invested in a funded occupational or personal pension, the aim should be to increase the proportion of NICs invested in a fund designed to provide a combination of savings and insurance to meet a wide variety of life-cycle needs. Contributors should, of course, be able to choose from a range of properly regulated providers.

A first step could be taken in this direction by allowing approved pension schemes to offer provision for long-term care needs. Subsequently, they could offer a tax-relieved savings vehicle for other needs than simply retirement. Within appropriate limits, contributors to a pension scheme should be able to draw down on their accumulated fund for 'retirement before retirement' – in other words, for a period of parental or carers' leave, or for a learning sabbatical. Pension schemes would start to resemble 'time banks', allowing people to save more flexibly across increasingly varied life cycles. In the Canadian province of British Columbia, for instance, public sector employees can save up to a quarter of their salary in a special fund on which they can draw to take a period of leave, protected by a reinstatement right.

As noted earlier, the present structure of employers' NICs creates an artificial incentive to employers to transform full-time into part-time jobs, with a damaging effect on Treasury revenues. On the other hand, the lower rate of taxation on lower earnings may encourage job creation for less-skilled workers who are most likely to be unemployed and, for that reason, is precisely the structure that the European Commission is urging other countries to adopt as part of its employment programme. The answer, ideally, is to graduate employers' NICs according to hourly pay, rather than total weekly earnings. Such a change would, however, impose considerable administrative demands on employers.

Provision of services

Time off for parents from employment should itself be part of a policy for child care. But an extension of services is also essential – not only to meet the needs of employed parents, but above all to meet the needs of growing children for social contact, pre-school education and safe, out-of-school care. Child-care and education services should not, however, be based on the assumption that all parents work or want to work full-time, although they should certainly recognise that some do. Thus, flexible services are required which can offer everything from a full-day place for 48 weeks of the year, through a variety of part-time places, to a short-notice place for an employed parent whose hours of work have suddenly been changed. Although local child-care partnerships should be created between local authorities, employers, parents and voluntary organisations, and every effort should be made (for instance, via planning gain) to mobilise private funding for an expansion of facilities, additional public spending will undoubtedly be required.

Nearly 7 million people in the UK care for a sick or disabled relative, friend or neighbour; 1.5 million of them provide care for more than 20 hours per week. At the very least, carers – like those they look after – should be entitled to a needs assessment from local authorities, with respite care and other support provided where required. More fundamentally, the growing number of very elderly people – many of whom will require a substantial degree of domiciliary or residential care – inevitably poses a question of costs. Many of those costs today fall on friends and family. If, however, younger generations become less willing to give up employment for unpaid care, or if the strain of doing so becomes insupportable, the costs will have to be met elsewhere – whether from taxation for those entitled to means-tested care (assuming that the present trend away from providing such care within the NHS continues) or through a charge upon elderly people's assets, or both.

Conclusion

During the 1980s, part-time employment became the focus for an ideological battle. While neo-liberals saw the growth in part-time employment as an unqualified good – reducing costs, moderating wage rises and meeting women's desire for shorter working hours – on the left of the political spectrum, part-time employment symbolised the low-wage, low-value-added economy which they feared Britain was becoming. The truth is considerably more complex. Part-time employment has undoubtedly increased the working-time options available, meeting the needs not only of many women with young children but also some, at least, of those approaching retirement or with other calls upon their time. Despite the low pay which is still associated with part-time work, employees in these jobs consistently express higher satisfaction with their working conditions than full-time employees. And although part-time employment is still most often found in low-paid and lower-level occupations, it is beginning to be available in higher-paid and more responsible jobs as well.

At the same time, the labour market deregulation that has helped to promote part-time employment has permitted both an increase in the hours worked by full-time employees and a decline in the hours worked by some part-time employees: unlimited hours at one end of the spectrum, zero hours at the other. At both extremes, unacceptable risks are imposed upon employees and, in some cases, upon third parties as well. Furthermore, a 'lumpy' playing field – the result of employment and social security systems designed originally for a world of full-time employment – has created incentives to distort working-hour arrangements to fit the regulatory system, rather than the needs of enterprises and employees.

The United Kingdom's regulatory regime is, however, only one of the factors accounting for the growth in part-time employment. More important, in the drivers of change, are the shifts in technology, production systems and family patterns which are shaping post-industrial economies. Part-time employment is here to stay, as part of a growing variety of working patterns and working life cycles. Viewed from this perspective, 'flexible' employment offers an opportunity to achieve both greater efficiency for enterprises and greater autonomy for individuals in combining, in different ways at different stages of their lives, the demands of employment, family, learning and leisure. If that opportunity is to be seized, the deregulation of the 1980s needs to give way to a new, strategic regulatory approach which will eliminate unacceptable extremes and, above all, open up new options for managers and workers alike.

Notes

1. Data for 1983, the 'trough' year, are not available.

2. For a full review of the evidence, see Hewitt (1993).

3. According to the Winter 93/94 Labour Force Survey, 89 per cent of women and 72 per cent of men working part-time do not want a full-time job.

4. It should, however, be noticed that the 'parenting deficit' identified by

Etzioni is, in this country, largely a 'fathering' and not a 'mothering' deficit.

5. See the Commission on Social Justice report, Chapter 6, for further details on the creation of part-time benefits.

References

Bassett, P. (1994) 'Part-time solutions that mask full-time problems', *The Times*, 18 April

Butcher, S. and Hart, D. (1995). 'An analysis of working time 1979–1994', *Employment Gazette*, May

Commission on Social Justice (1994) *Social Justice: Strategies for National Renewal*, Vintage

Etzioni, A. (1994) *The Parenting Deficit*, DEMOS 1994

European Commission (1993) *Employment in Europe 1993*, CEC

Field, F. (1995) *Making Welfare Work*, Institute of Community Studies

Hakim, C. (1989) 'Workforce restructuring, social insurance coverage and the black economy', *Journal of Social Policy*, vol. 18, no. 4, pp. 471–503

Hewitt, P. (1993) *About Time: The Revolution in Work and Family Life*, IPPR/Rivers Oram

Hewlett, S. A. (1991) *When the Bough Breaks*, Basic Books, New York

Hidden (1989) *Investigation into the Clapham Junction Railway Accident*, Department of Transport, HMSO

Kamerman, S. and Kahn A. (eds) (1991) *Child Care, Parental Leave and the Under 3s: Policy Innovation in Europe*, Auburn House, Connecticut

McRae, S. (1993) 'Returning to work after childbirth: opportunities and inequalities', *European Sociological Review*, vol. 9, no. 2

Marsh, C. (1991) *Hours of Work of Women and Men in Britain*, Equal Opportunities Commission, HMSO, London

TUC (1995) *The Pros and Cons of Part-time Working*, March

Witherspoon, S. and Prior, G. (1991) 'Working mothers: free to choose?', in R. Jowell *et al* (eds) *British Social Attitudes, 8th Report,* SCPR, Dartmouth

4 The labour market and risk

Michael White

Introduction

This review of labour market developments is organised around one concept: risk. There are two reasons for this choice of perspective. First, by thinking about risk one can begin to see changes in the labour market, and other social changes, as part of a single process. Second, the combined risks which people face may influence their decisions in any one respect. If, as many believe, the employment relationship is becoming increasingly insecure, this is likely to have implications for the risks people bear in their lives as a whole, and for how they handle risk.

The major part of this chapter is devoted to a discussion of whether, or how, the labour market is becoming more risky. This is preceded by an introductory discussion of risk as a general social tendency. The discussion of change in the labour market is followed by brief examples of the connection of labour market risk to some current social changes and problems.

Risk in the market era

In common speech, risk is used in (at least) two related but distinct senses. In one sense, risk is simply the probability that a bad or undesired outcome will occur, for example the risk of being killed if one is in a war zone. In the other sense, risk is the down-side of actions or situations which also have an up-side; in other words, risk is variation in outcomes, usually weighted by their probabilities. A risky investment offers a chance of high returns but also of losses. A risk-averse person is one who is more deterred by possible losses than attracted by the associated possible gains. It is in the second sense – wide and uncertain variation in outcomes – that this chapter will consider risk.

In the past decade or so, sociologists, especially in Germany (see for example, Beck, 1992), have developed a theory of 'risk society' which argues that there has been a pervasive increase in social risks that stems from the advance of competitive market systems and the individualistic behaviour associated with them. This theory is valuable in three ways:

- It suggests that one should consider changes in risk across different fields, such as employment relations and family relations, rather than in isolation.

- It puts forward a common explanation for increasing risks.

- It stresses individual awareness of risks and resulting changes in life strategies, over and above the actuarial estimation of risk.

The view of risk which I propose has been influenced by these ideas, but also has a different emphasis in several respects. In particular, I would stress the importance of social values in producing change, and accordingly see the advance of competitive market society – and the risks involved in that advance – as partly created by networks of related choices, rather than imposed hierarchically or from outside. As an economist might put it, risk is endogenous not exogenous. Further, social actors will continually be attempting to change society and to modify risks in particular areas; hence, changes in risk are not necessarily either uniform or unidirectional. In less formal language, competitive market society, with its risks, has developed because many people valued what it provided or was expected to provide; but if people can find ways of getting the up-side without the down-side, they will strive to do so. Further, some people may succeed in limiting the risks for themselves while gaining access to the benefits, while for others the reverse may apply. The distributive aspect is all the more important when, as in a risky society, the range of outcomes is wide.

How, then, can one visualise risk being produced in a market society? One can do so by contrasting it with the more regulated type of economic and social order which existed previously (and in some respects continues to exist). People have sought greater variety in consumption, more freedom and self-actualisation in personal life and relationships, and, to underpin both, a higher material standard of living. Materialistic demands have created continuous pressure, or at least legitimation, for the dismantling of regulation in the economic sphere, so as to move closer to the productive potential of competitive markets. Demands for personal freedom or self-realisation have led to less standardised and constrained life courses, especially through the legal and social acceptance of divorce, the progressive though still incomplete removal of gender differences in life chances, the continuous critical reappraisal of received values or norms, and the diversification of working careers.

Regulation or standardisation, whether in industry and trade, social behaviour, the work career or life cycle, reduces the variation of outcomes and makes verything more predictable, though more constrained. In a risk society, utcomes have greater variation than previously, and may tend to become olarised because of the interconnectedness of risks. A society of risk offers ncreased freedom and opportunity to those who through talent or luck can naster the dangers or rise to the remaining safe ground, but it may leave others nore exposed to disaster. Further, the development of a competitive market ociety, with its attendant values, tends to threaten some of the institutions vhich formerly protected individuals. For example, welfare benefits may come nder attack, because they appear to subvert the discipline of the market or lace a demotivating burden on the enterprising. Family obligations or ommunity solidarity may crumble as individualistic lifestyles predominate. ach person may increasingly be thrown back on her or his own strategy for oping with risks, as external supports themselves become at risk.

Widening risk in the British labour market?

now dwell in more detail upon the labour market. For this purpose I first onsider Britain, where more detailed information is to hand. Having haracterised the British development, I turn to some broad contrasts with other uropean countries. The questions to be addressed throughout are:

What kinds of risk are there in the labour market?

How are they changing?

Who bears them?

Competitive pressures

ince I have stressed the competitive background to the labour market, it is ppropriate to begin with a few indications of this. The growth of international ompetition is of central importance: as world capacity grows and barriers to rade are reduced, comparative advantage is given more scope and the weaker ational industries or firms are forced out of existence. The result is that a reater proportion of each economy consists in overseas trade; the extent to vhich this has already taken place, and is expected to continue, is shown in igure 4.1.

ompetition at the level of the organisation is experienced in terms both of rices and non-price factors. The results of a large survey in 1986–87 are shown n Table 4.1; they show that most organisations were experiencing increasing ompetitive pressures. Although it is sometimes said that non-price competition

Figure 4.1 Overseas trade and the UK economy, 1970–1990–2010

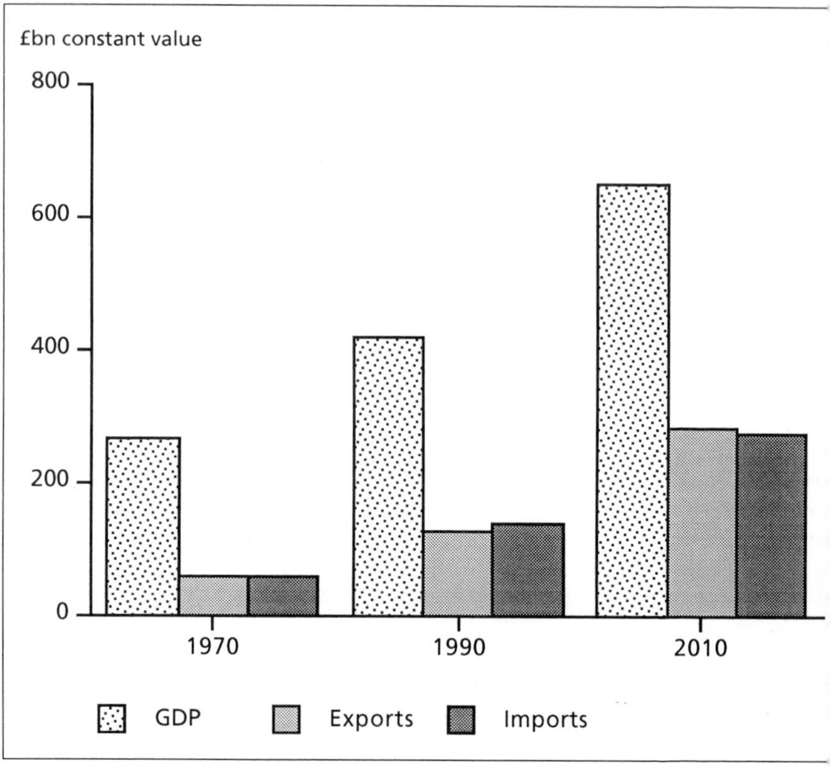

£bn constant value

Source: Cambridge Econometrics

Table 4.1 Competitive pressures in private and public sectors (%)

Private sector

Increased customer selectivity on quality or standards of service	84
Increased customer selectivity on price	84

Public sector

Requirement for higher standards of service	82
Pressure from changing financial requirements of Government	89

Source: Wilkinson and White (1994); based on establishments with at least 20 employees, SCELI survey

quality or service) has displaced price competition, this is evidently not correct; rather, price competition and non-price competition are felt about equally. Notably, such pressures were felt as much or more in public sector organisations as in the market sector.

An analysis using the same data showed that the existence and type of competitive pressures had widespread effects on employers' labour policies (Wilkinson and White, 1994). Notably, increasing price pressures were strongly related to the implementation of workforce reductions. Where workforce reductions had taken place, the satisfaction with job security of employees was markedly reduced (White and Gallie, 1994). There was therefore a linkage between competitive price pressure and an increased sense of individual insecurity. This was not so with non-price competition.

Pressure on jobs is one way of expressing competition between firms; another is pressure to increase wages and salaries. Figure 4.2 is a familiar chart from the OECD and depicts the simple relationship between wage rigidity and unemployment. The UK comes out in the top right corner of the chart, as a high-unemployment country where wage increases are not moderated in the face of unemployment. At a less abstract level, Figure 4.3 shows how, over many years, the average rate of wage increases in Britain has kept ahead of the rate of inflation; the two curves intersect only briefly at the depths of the last two major recessions.

The recent history of wages illustrates, in part, the concept of risk in the labour market: the average employee was able to increase her or his earnings, even while unemployment was affecting many others (and the same person may be both a winner and a loser in this game, at different times). Wage pressure is also part of the institutional mechanism that produces risk. The inflationary pressures coming from wages are held in check by governments' restrictive economic policies, which prevent the full productive potential of society from being expressed. As a result, many people are inevitably forced into unemployment or underemployment.

Assessing risk in the labour market

To assess risk in a systematic way, one would have to take each initial decision, event or state, consider the outcomes which follow, and carry out appropriate comparisons. An obvious place to start is by taking an initial employment position and considering whether it leads to stable employment or to unemployment. Another risk that it would be desirable to assess is whether an initial employment position leads to high (stable) or low (unstable) earnings. Despite

Figure 4.2 Real wage rigidity and unemployment

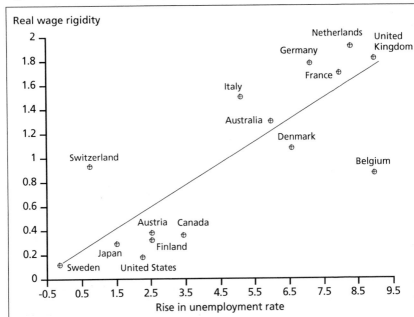

Note: The unemployment measure is change in the percentage rate between 1973 and 1987.

Source: Economies in Transition, *OECD (1989)*

the large amount of information about earnings which is available, very little of it concerns variability for individuals over time or the dispersions in earnings for particular groups.[1] As a fairly poor substitute, we can use average earnings, or we might consider what the chances are of moving to a better-rewarded or a worse-rewarded position.

In what follows, I do not attempt to analyse risk in a formal way. Rather, I very informally review some of the main tendencies in the labour market which can give us a more judgemental, intuitive feel for how risk is developing.

Unemployment
How risky is unemployment itself? By the tests just outlined, it is – in Britain – very risky indeed. While the majority of entrants to unemployment have

Figure 4.3 Average earnings and retail prices – United Kingdom

Note: Earnings data are seasonally adjusted and for Great Britain only.

Source: Central Statistical Office, Employment Department, Social Trends 1995

returned to employment within six months, the average period to exit is about one year, and a substantial minority have very long unemployment periods. Further, one spell of unemployment tends to lead to another (Daniel, 1990; Tomlinson, 1994; Gershuny and Marsh, 1994). While some people can resume their careers, for many others they are completely disrupted. Even for those getting back into jobs, the path of earnings also frequently receives a setback; several studies have reported post-unemployment real earnings that were lower than those before unemployment (Daniel, 1990; White and McRae, 1989).

Much more conspicuous is the loss of income during unemployment, by comparison with remaining employed. For most people in Britain, unemployment results in a sharp reduction of income. If continuing beyond the short-term, this leads to reduced material living standards, a high level of financial anxiety, debt, family tensions, and psychological stress.[2] Other contributions in this volume (see Chapters 5 and 7) discuss this aspect in depth.

More positions in the labour market are becoming at risk of unemployment. In the 1970s and 1980s, the risk of unemployment (especially long-term unemployment) was borne chiefly by manual workers and by women in routine non-manual work. While this remains true to a great degree, in the early 1990s there were sharp relative increases in the redundancy and unemployment of white-collar employees, especially those in professional occupations and in professional service industries (see Hasluck and Green, 1994). It is hazardous to predict whether these tendencies will continue. However, the scope for rationalising manual jobs may have diminished because so many of them went in the last three recessions. By the next recession, say in the early 2000s, employers seeking to rationalise would for that reason be more likely to focus on white-collar workers; and the advance of information technology would support this.[3]

The widening spread of unemployment becomes still more apparent if one examines it by age group, as in Table 4.2. Of the men aged under 30 at the time of the 1990s recession, 45 per cent had already had at least one spell of unemployment; among women aged under 30, the proportion was one-third. These are larger proportions than experienced *over their whole working life* by older age groups up to the same date. For recent waves of labour market entrants, unemployment at some time is near to being the normal expectation, whereas for earlier waves it was uncommon.

Table 4.2 Prevalence of unemployment experience in careers to 1992 (%)

Men	20–29	30–39	40–49	50–59	All
Never unemployed	55	56	64	67	59
Unemployed once or more often	45	44	36	33	41
Women	**20–29**	**30–39**	**40–49**	**50–59**	**All**
Never unemployed	67	70	75	77	72
Unemployed once or more often	33	30	25	23	28

Source: Tomlinson (1994), adapted

Subjective insecurity

Information from a national survey of 1992,[4] at the depths of the recession, confirmed that even among those who had not lost their jobs, insecurity was widespread. Half of men and 43 per cent of women in employment had witnessed a reduction in numbers employed at their workplace in the previous two years; 42 per cent of men, and 31 per cent of women, felt that their personal job security had declined over the previous five years;[5] over three-quarters of each sex felt that it would be difficult, or very difficult, to get a comparable job if they lost their present one.

Destandardised employment

While unemployment is the primary source of risk in the labour market, other positions may be risky either in leading into unemployment or in fostering other types of unwanted outcome, such as reduced earnings. A popular way of classifying labour market positions is in terms of their contractual status. Casual work, homeworking, temporary jobs, fixed-term contracts, part-time jobs, and self-employment have all been considered precarious, hence increasing risk. Indeed, Ulrich Beck (1992) emphasises 'destandardised employment', rather than unemployment *per se*, as the key risk concept of the labour market.

This view, however, seems to rest on a legalistic definition of reality: because destandardised jobs are less protected in labour law, they are considered more risky. This is inadequate if risk is defined in terms of outcomes. It is necessary to identify the particular forms of employment relationship which lead to specific types of risk, rather than assume a simple dichotomy between 'standard' and 'destandardised' forms.

Short-term temporary jobs in Britain seldom have beneficial characteristics (e.g. in terms of earnings or training opportunities) for their holders (White and Gallie, 1994). Strangely, no rigorous analysis has been carried out, in Britain, of the risk of entering or remaining in unemployment following a temporary job. However, around 15–25 per cent of unemployed people report coming from a previous job that was temporary (whereas temporary jobs are only around 5 per cent of all employment). People who have been unemployed also have a greatly increased chance of moving into jobs of this type (Payne and Payne, 1993), which suggests that the two states form a kind of trap. However, during the 1980s there was no growth in temporary employment as a whole, and no growth in the relative share of temporary employment taken by recently unemployed people (Payne and Payne, 1993). Temporary employment therefore appeared to be an important part of labour market risk, but it was not a growing part. However, many employers now say that they expect to make more use of temporary contracts in the future (CBI, 1994). If this happens without change in the characteristics of this type of work, the consequence is likely to be that more people will be trapped in a cycle of unemployment and insecure, low-paid work without development opportunities.

Short-term temporary contracts should not be confused with *fixed-term contracts* of one to three years, which are chiefly used among qualified professional and technical workers. Such employment,[6] while increasing exposure to unemployment, may offer compensating advantages in terms of earnings, career variety, or accelerated learning. But to get these advantages, people have to perform competitively and some may lose in the process while others gain. A good case study is provided by the decentralisation of the broadcasting industry, details of which are summarised in Box 4.1. Change has evidently led to increased rewards for many broadcasting professionals, but has also pushed many others towards the status of casual workers. There is insufficient information[7] to discern any economy-wide trend towards increased contract working, but the developments in the broadcasting industry could be repeated in other industries with a high professional content, in response to competition and deregulation.

The huge growth of *self-employment* in Britain during the 1980s could be regarded as strong evidence of growing exposure to risk in the labour market. Two problems in verifying this are, first, that data on the incomes of self-employed people are not reliable and, second, that there are different types of self-employment with varying exposures to risks. Much of the contract working which has just been discussed could also be classified as self-employment. Much professional self-employment (e.g. medicine and accountancy) is traditional,

---

The growth of contract working in broadcasting

The growth of local radio, the installation of Channel 4 TV (with all programmes made by independent producers), Government intervention to enforce contracting-out of programmes by the BBC, and the internal rationalisation of the BBC in the face of competitive and deregulatory pressures, have in combination led to a massive shift away from the standard employment relation towards temporary employment or service contracts. More than half of production work and directly related services is now fulfilled by freelances and independent producers, across the whole industry.[8]

In a survey of freelance workers, the reasons given for becoming freelance were a mixture of choice and constraint.[9] Some 42 per cent noted 'greater freedom', 26 per cent worked freelance to improve earnings, 26 per cent for 'better quality work', and 17 per cent for promotion; but 35 per cent did it because they had been made redundant or expected to be made redundant, and 16 per cent because it was the only work available.

The same survey revealed that there was also a wide dispersion of outcomes for freelances. The mean number of days worked in the previous year was 173 – with 42 per cent working 200 or more days, but 31 per cent working less than 130 days and 14 per cent working less than 70.

---

egulated and secure. At the other extreme is self-employment in small-scale
etailing, building services or personal services, which may be highly exposed to
ailure and attract many people wanting to escape unemployment. This type of
mall-business self-employment experienced a setback in the recession of the
arly 1990s, resulting in bankruptcies, financial losses and more unemployment.

)n the other hand, it is not obvious whether, *when moving from unemployment*,
elf-employment increases or reduces risk by comparison with the poor-quality
)bs that may be the main alternatives. A recent analysis showed that, after long-
erm unemployment, the stability of self-employment was greater than that of
ull-time jobs in the period 1990–92. Consistent with this, the entrants to self-
mployment expressed more risk-averse attitudes (Bryson and White, 1995).
\ full risk evaluation, however, would have to take account of the financial
onsequences of self-employed failure by comparison with the failure of
mployment (including financial losses and further effects on employment
hances).

art-time employment has frequently been represented as both precarious and
isadvantaged. It has been by far the largest section of destandardised
mployment, and has been a substantial area of continuing growth even in the
990s. The argument that risk results from destandardisation rests heavily on
he assessment of part-time work. As with temporary work, people (both
vomen and men) who have recently been unemployed have an added
)robability of entering part-time work, and also of saying that they do so for
ack of a full-time job opportunity (Payne and Payne, 1993). However, this only
dds to risk if the part-time jobs (like temporary ones) soon lead back into
inemployment, so that a kind of trap develops.

'his does not seem to be the case. A recent analysis of the stability of jobs after
)ng-term unemployment has shown that part-time jobs were more, not less,
table than full-time jobs for people with this background (Bryson and White,
995). Another detailed analysis has shown that, in 1986–87, part-time work on
verage was rather secure, and perceived as such by those who held part-time
)bs (White and Gallie, 1994). Average hourly earnings, too, were not
isadvantageous compared to full-time jobs, when 'human capital' and the
maller tax-wedge faced by part-timers were taken into account. The main
isadvantage of part-time work was its reduced access to training and to
romotion opportunities, by comparison with full-time work.

)verall, the role of destandardised employment contracts in risk is harder to
ssess than one might assume. The clearest addition to risk would occur if short-

term temporary or contract work increased. At present, such jobs represent only about 5 per cent of the British labour market, but experience elsewhere in Europe suggests that growth can be rapid. In addition, there is still very poor information about the real risks involved in self-employment, how they arise and how they are distributed. There is a particular need to assess this more carefully, because of the potential for a large further growth in self-employment

The changing employment relation in 'standard' employment

Since about two-thirds of jobs are full-time and permanent, the conditions unde which these jobs are held can make a great difference to the prevalent level of risk. Potentially, all the personnel policies of employers can affect the degree of risk, either by (directly or indirectly) changing the probability of severance and unemployment, or by increasing or narrowing the variability in earnings and prospects.

Large proportions – around half – of those entering unemployment arrive there through closures or redundancies. Employers' rationalisation policies are therefore important. A new element in this has been 'delayering', that is the removal of management, supervision or other intermediate jobs, which may have been practised by around one in five firms in the last recession (Storey et a 1993). The persistent effort of employers, over the past 15 years, to change working practices, reorganise work, and introduce new technology, is also connected with a continuing pruning of numbers. Rationalisation has been particularly marked in the privatised industries and services.

Another response of employers to competitive pressures might be to cut back directly on pay and employee benefits. In the USA, the imposition of less-favourable pay and benefits has been commonplace since the 1980s (Harrison and Bluestone, 1988). For example, most airline companies resorted to this form of cost reduction in the wake of deregulation (Gialloretto, 1988). This approach, however, seems rare in Britain and in Europe generally, despite a few well-publicised cases to the contrary.

British employers appear particularly dependent on what Amitai Etzioni label-led 'remunerative power' (Etzioni, 1975) to obtain compliance from employees, especially if they are pressing forward with change that they wish to legitimate. This, in combination with the desire of employees to advance their living standards, helps to explain the way in which wage pressure has remained high despite mass unemployment. Nor is the small-firm sector sharply defined in terms of lower wages; size tends to be weakly or non-significantly related to earnings in wage equations which control for 'human capital' (White and Gallie

994). However, while protecting employees against earnings risk, these wage policies create or exacerbate unemployment risk. This is most simply seen in the direct association between size of wage increases and propensity to rationalise the workforce, at workplace level (Ingram, 1991).

Similar observations apply to benefits. Although minor 'perks' have often been pruned in recent years, there have been substantial advances in the larger and more expensive benefits, notably pensions. For example, both the accrual rates of pensions and the inflation-proofing of pension payments were improved in the majority of occupational schemes during the 1980s (Government Actuary's Department, 1991; National Association of Pension Funds, 1993). By the early 1990s, occupational pension schemes were available to 61 per cent of employees, and sick pay schemes (above the statutory level) to 57 per cent (Gallie and White, 1993). So, in terms of the central benefits, employers were continuing to protect the majority of established employees against some common types of risk. At the same time as 'insiders' benefit from these protections, however, there is a static or worsening provision for the 'outsiders', for example through the capping or reduction of the public welfare benefits which are their analogous provision.

Another important, and widely remarked, feature of employer policy has been the 'individualisation' of rewards. It is true that, by the early 1990s, the older type of incentive or commission scheme was being applied only to about one in five employees, and frequently with small cash values involved (Gallie and White, 1993). At the same time, however, more than half the workforce had become covered by some combination of personal performance appraisal, target setting and merit pay – a combination now often referred to as 'performance management'. Thus the great majority of employees (and this is especially so in larger organisations) are covered by systems which assess performance in one way or another, and adjust rewards or progression on this basis.

The 'performance management' systems appear to be successful in increasing employee satisfaction and motivation (Gallie et al, forthcoming), and their increasing adoption therefore appears probable. They promise employees better chances of having their contribution recognised and rewarded. However, if recognition and reward are defined in financial terms, it seems likely that such systems will also have a down-side that will increase risk. If rewards are increased for some, while average rewards remain the same, then they must be decreased for others; the decrease may in some cases take the form of the employer identifying and 'eliminating' unsatisfactory performers. Alternatively, if rewards are increased for some, without being decreased for others, then performance management systems will probably contribute to the wage inflationary pressures referred to before.[10]

As part of an increasingly dominant ethic of individual reward, increasingly large payments are being made to senior executives, 'high flyers' or those with scarce talents, and those working in elite organisations. Once more, these high rewards are likely to be accommodated either by squeezing down the rewards of others who are less successful or fortunate, or by contributing to inflationary pressures.[11]

Apart from pay, the most important area of corporate personnel policies, in terms of economic and social consequences, is training and development. When the continuity of jobs seems uncertain, and there may be a need to be mobile, individuals would be well advised to have portable and flexible skills and qualifications. But if employers expect larger proportions of their employees to move on, then they may not be willing to provide the training needed by individuals.

Nonetheless it appears that there was, in the late 1980s and early 1990s, a marked increase in the *continuing*[12] vocational education and training provided, with 54 per cent of employees obtaining such training during the 1990–92 period, by comparison with 33 per cent in 1984–86 (Gallie and White, 1993). Further, the average duration of continuing training increased over the comparison period. The chief purpose was apparently to respond to higher skill demands in the majority of jobs, including (but by no means limited to) those resulting from new technology. At the same time, some employers also began enunciating an explicit policy of providing training to employees as a means of preparing them for exit from their current employment. This is called the 'employability' principle, since such employers are withdrawing a commitment to long-term employment of their workforce, but replacing it with a commitment to equip them for employment elsewhere (see Waterman, Waterman and Collard, 1994).

Thus, at first sight the recent development of training provision would appear to reduce the riskiness of the labour market by improving average outcomes on termination of a job. As always, however, one must consider the distributive and relative effects as well as the direct effects. Here the evidence is less reassuring, since training has been concentrated on those who are already in relatively strong positions, such as managers and professionals, those with prior (especially advanced) educational qualifications, those working with advanced technology, and those experiencing upskilling and increased responsibility

(Gallie and White, 1993). Conversely, those who tend to miss out on training are semi-skilled and non-skilled manual workers, those without any educational qualifications, and those in short-term temporary jobs – precisely the categories where the risk of unemployment is endemic.

The general tendency of employers' policies in Britain seems reasonably clear. Any presumption of security of employment has been withdrawn, either explicitly or implicitly, and a continuous rationalisation of labour is proceeding. But for those employees able to retain 'insider' positions, a very positive climate of reward and recognition has been created through policies on pay, benefits, performance management and training. This combination of policies is likely to stimulate individualistic, competitive behaviour, and increase overall risk in the labour market through its aggregate effects on unemployment and its distributional effects, especially on excluded 'outsiders'.

Labour market risk in Europe

The purpose of this section is to extend the discussion of labour market risk to Europe.[13] I first abstract a few broad themes from the British case, and then look at some similarities and contrasts among the countries of the European Union.[14] An underlying assumption is that all the societies and their labour markets are facing roughly similar pressures from the development of competitive market systems.[15] But the pressures work through in different ways, because of the specificities of each society. To carry out this comparative task in few words, the treatment that follows is inevitably schematic.

The labour market can be characterised in terms of three sections: unemployment, destandardised employment, and the standard employment relationship. The pressures created by the development of competitive market society can be expressed in various combinations across these three sections. In addition, there may be important horizontal divisions of the standard employment relationship, as for instance between white-collar and manual workers, elite and non-elite workers, or native and immigrant workers, depending on the country.

In Britain, most of the pressure on the labour market is expressed in the links between unemployment and the standard employment relationship. Labour market risk has been increased through change in the standard relationship, which has been made easier by the lack of external regulation of employment. The employment relationship has discarded much of its protective function (which was largely customary), employers have used remunerative power to achieve progressive rationalisation, and surplus labour has been pushed out into unemployment. The destandardised sector has had little independent role in Britain; different parts of it have served as appendages to the standard employment relationship (part-time contracts) or to unemployment (temporary contracts, perhaps parts of self-employment).

In other EU countries, except Denmark and Ireland, the standard employment relationship is subjected to a greater degree of external regulation than in Britain, and to continuing intervention by the State. The standard employment relationship remains somewhat more protective, destandardised employment plays a larger role in the transmission of risk, and there is a higher risk of total exclusion, notably for women and for new entrants. One of the clearest indications of these differences is the fact that Britain is the only EU country, except Ireland, where the female unemployment rate is considerably lower than the male. In addition, youth unemployment in Britain has been relatively low and its youth employment rate has been exceeded only by Denmark. The low level of temporary employment in Britain can be seen in Figure 4.4.

Figure 4.4 Temporary employment in the European Union, 1987 and 1991

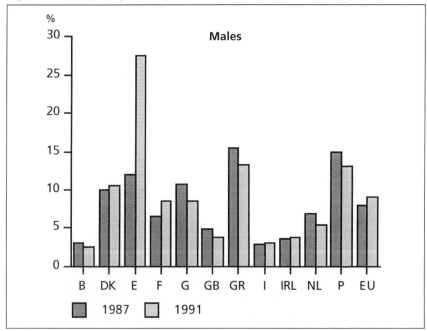

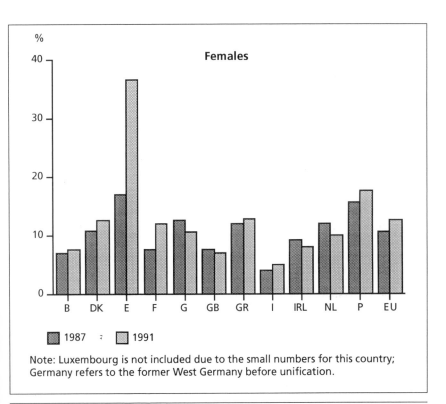

Note: Luxembourg is not included due to the small numbers for this country; Germany refers to the former West Germany before unification.

Source: Eurostat/Steiner (1994)

These generalisations must immediately be qualified. Several of the northern countries of Europe – highly regulated Germany and the Netherlands, as well as less-regulated Ireland – appear to have more in common with Britain, in terms of how labour market risk is distributed, than with other countries. Indicators of this are the age structure of unemployment, and especially the fact that, in these four countries only, unemployment falls more on heads of household than on others in the household. This suggests that in all four countries, unemployment is the result of a process of rationalisation affecting the standard employment relationship, and hence dispossessing established prime-age workers of their jobs. It would seem that, in Germany and the Netherlands, employer policies are capable of overriding external regulation. In this they may be assisted by welfare provision, which is at a more generous level than in Britain or Ireland and so eases the way to acceptance of rationalisation.

As in Britain, the destandardised section of employment appears to be quite well integrated with the permanent employment sector in the Netherlands and to a lesser extent in Germany. In the Netherlands, part-time employment has been greatly expanded as women increased their labour market participation, and also as port of entry to the labour market for young people. Its effects seem in general benign. In Germany there is little part-time employment, but temporary employment has been deliberately expanded through deregulation, to create flexibility. A recent analysis (V. Steiner, summarised in Gallie, 1994) has indicated that, in Germany, the role of temporary employment has been risk-reducing: those who enter it (primarily young people) tend to enter standard permanent employment at the next step, rather than falling back into unemployment. Available information on the Netherlands indicates that temporary employment works in the same way there.

Destandardised employment plays larger, and very different, roles in the countries of the EU which border the Mediterranean. There is a much clearer segmentation between primary or standard employment, which remains somewhat protected by law and custom alike, and the destandardised sector which provides much of the flexibility and absorbs much of the risk. But this concentration of risk on the destandardised sector also makes many people reluctant to enter it; they prefer to wait, as long as possible, for an opening in the more advantageous primary sector.[16] In several of these countries, most unemployment is made up of young people or women attempting to enter the labour market. Discrimination in the labour market against women generally remains strong, and average periods of unemployment are very long. As always, these generalisations need to be tempered by attending to country-specific differences. I will briefly consider two countries, France and Spain, and then Italy at somewhat greater length as it provides a particularly clear contrast with the British case.

France is in many respects an anomalous case, with some features more like Britain or Germany, while others are more like the southern countries. The standard employment form, though regulated and protected, has not prevented substantial rationalisation; the State has cushioned this partly by massive early retirement provisions. Part-time employment has been regulated in such a way that it is well integrated with the standard employment form; for example, train-ing provision is more even-handed for part-time and full-time employees than in Britain. Consistent with continuing regulation, unemployment falls heavily on women. Flexibility has been provided mainly through the increasing level of temporary employment, which appears to be closely bound to unemployment and offers rather poor chances of transition to standard, stable employment.

pain has rapidly been constructing a modern competitive economy, but part of he foundation is a traditional dual labour market with a protected and regula- ed primary sector. Unemployment, and especially long-term unemployment, as been high and heavily concentrated on women, who have been attempting o increase their economic participation. To increase flexibility, the State ermitted an unregulated growth of employment on short-term temporary ontracts. There was then an explosive growth in the temporary sector, which eached more than 25 per cent of male employment, and more than 35 per cent f female employment, by 1991.

he case of Italy has been particularly well explained in a number of papers by milio Reyneri (for example, Reyneri, 1994). Italy has a good claim to be the nost regulated labour market in Europe. The employment relationship has emained for the most part long-term and stable. Further, structural edundancies have been smoothed out by a unique benefit fund, the *Cassa ntegrazione Guadagni* (CIG), which has provided around 90 per cent of normal arnings for displaced workers *without them giving up their employed status.*[17])nly 5 per cent of the Italian job seekers are men who have lost a job. There is lso little destandardised employment; most flexibility has been provided by the elf-employed sector, which has been large but is now shrinking.

fost unemployment in Italy is concentrated on young people (new entrants to he labour market) and, to a lesser extent, on married women attempting to nter or return. Periods of unemployment are typically very long. Yet Italy has he lowest level, in Europe, of *household* unemployment (that is, of households vhere at least one person is unemployed and nobody is employed), and also the owest unemployment rate among heads of household.

\ most important factor has been the role of the family and of social attitudes. :hildren in Italy normally remain in the parental home until marriage, and not nfrequently for some time after, whether or not they have employment. \ccordingly, a prolonged period of dependence on the family is not a peculiar problem of unemployed youth. The strength of family relations provides many :inds of practical support, including opportunities to work in the household :conomy or informal economy. Reyneri reports that only 13 per cent of inemployed people live in poverty, as defined in Italy, and they constitute only i per cent of all those so classified.

fowever, Italy is an international market economy, with a materialistic culture, ınd it thereby faces the same pressures as elsewhere in Europe. The Italian velfare system, which has been important in protecting non-competitive aspects of the labour market, is on the verge of collapse and has already been cut back repeatedly during the 1990s. Public employment has also been a crucial prop of the old system and is now unsustainable. It is hard to see how prime-aged unemployment can then be restrained, in the face of already strong wage pressures arising from high aspirations.

It seems, then, that while a country may to some extent control the distribution or form of labour market risk, it cannot evade that risk altogether. If some other European countries now seem to have less risky labour markets than Britain, that difference may be either deceptive or fragile. When regulation gives way suddenly, it often releases a particularly turbulent period of change. In the USA, the deregulation of banking, transport and telecommunications led to far more severe price wars, and deeper rationalisation and restructuring of the labour force, than most people could imagine in advance (Bleeke, 1993). The next decade could witness a considerable increase in risky labour markets in Europe, as major industries (telecommunications, air transport, financial services) become deregulated and as public policies shift in the direction of 'flexibility' and budgetary cuts rather than protection.

The labour market and social risks

The preceding discussion of risks in the labour market has to be connected with wider social risks if we are to understand the problems and decisions facing individuals. How do risks accumulate across employment and other aspects of individuals' lives? This final section has the modest aim of illustrating some of the possible connections, with the aid of some recent findings.

A start is provided by a study by Serge Paugam (1994), covering six countries of the European Union. Paugam first constructed an indicator, which he calls *precariousness*, ranging from a stable permanent job (little or no disadvantage) to long-term unemployment (severe disadvantage), with various degrees of temporary or unstable employment and short-term unemployment in between. He then identified 11 statistical relationships with other social conditions, which are summarised in Tables 4.3–4.5. The initial point to note is that all the relationships are significant for some or all of the countries. Paugam stresses that these relationships are simplistic, and require much more intensive analysis; their function is to suggest directions of further investigation.

Of particular interest is the correlation between precariousness and (lack of) marital relationship. Nobody would suggest that precariousness of employment is a chief cause of changing patterns of family formation, or vice versa, but

Table 4.3 Correlations between precariousness of employment and weakness of social bonds, by country

	Single, separated/ divorced	Weak family relations	Low social activity	Low access to help
France	++	++	++	++
Britain	++	+	++	++
Netherlands	++	0	++	0
Denmark	++	++	++	0
Italy	++	—	NA	0
Spain	++	0	NA	—

Key
++   positive relation, p < 0.01
+   positive relation, p < 0.05
—   negative relation, p < 0.01
-     negative relation, p < 0.05
0   no correlation
NA   no data

Source: Paugam (1994), own translation

Table 4.4 Correlations between precariousness of employment and deprived living conditions, by country

	Low household income	Low standard of accommodation	Low standard of furnishings	Poor environment
France	++	++	++	++
Britain	++	+	++	++
Netherlands	++	++	++	NA
Denmark	++	++	++	++
Italy	++	NA	NA	NA
Spain	+	NA	0	0

Key
++   positive relation, p < 0.01
+   positive relation, p < 0.05
—   negative relation, p < 0.01
-     negative relation, p < 0.05
0   no correlation
NA   no data

Source: Paugam (1994), own translation

Table 4.5 Correlations between precariousness of employment and other disadvantages, by country

	Dependence on welfare	Poor health	Problems during youth
France	++	++	++
Britain	++	+	++
Netherlands	++	++	NA
Denmark	++	++	0
Italy	NA	NA	NA
Spain	NA	NA	NA

Key
++	positive relation, p < 0.01
+	positive relation, p < 0.05
—	negative relation, p < 0.01
-	negative relation, p < 0.05
0	no correlation
NA	no data

Source: Paugam (1994), own translation

various contributory links can be found in the literature. Young men unable to gain stable employment either defer marital partnership or are rejected as suitable partners (McRae, 1987). With a shortage of economically suitable male partners, some women may prefer to have children while remaining single;[18] once in this situation, a poverty trap may come into operation, preventing a return to the labour market. The loss of employment and decline in economic prospects may lead to marital breakdown (Lampard, 1994). Since the number of employed people in the household is one of the most powerful predictors of re-employment for unemployed people,[19] removal from the household and its associated jobs network is a serious practical handicap.

Also observed is an increase in long-term and life-long single status (see Mendras, 1990), and a greatly increased risk that those in this position will become long-term unemployed. This may suggest either that more people opt out of the standard life course (an aspect of 'individualisation'), or that with greater pressure on both the employment relation and the marital relation, there is more severe screening by personal traits in both domains.

One of the most visible social problems today is the homeless person living on the streets. A recent European study (Pieretti *et al*, 1993) concluded that this could not be explained simply as an extreme case of poverty. Family breakdown was often the core event, followed by abandonment of, or expulsion from, the home. But family breakdown, as just noted, may be partly a result of joblessness. In Britain, particularly, many homeless are poorly qualified young people who have poor prospects of steady employment. Again, the inability of individuals to cope with the situation may reflect their lack of human capital resources, limiting mobility in the job market (see Metcalf, 1994).

Recently published research on mortgage arrears or repossessions in Britain also confirms links with the labour market (Ford, Kempson and Wilson, 1995). In the first place, the deterioration of the housing market has been influenced by a climate of insecurity over jobs. Further, the occupational mix of those with severe mortgage problems looks little different from that of the whole economy, which is consistent with the spread of labour market risk to white-collar workers, as discussed earlier. Job loss and small-business failures are shown to be important reasons for mortgage-repayment problems, but this too is not simply a labour market problem, for family breakdown also appears to be a rapidly growing contributory factor.

These few examples, it is hoped, suggest how individuals or families are faced with an increasingly complex and pervasive combination of risks, coming from change in the labour market and from other aspects of social life. There are then two further sets of questions which the 'risk society' perspective leads towards.

The first set of questions, taking risk as given, concerns how people cope with it. Do they, for example, try to reduce risk or to bring it under their own control? Do they become gamblers or fatalists, or do they develop more complex life plans and strategies? How successful are their various approaches, in different circumstances?

The second set of questions concerns, more fundamentally, the social systems and policies which might help to reduce or contain risk. Is increased risk an inevitable, perhaps even a healthy, part of a competitive market society, or are there workable alternatives? As risk increases, should the welfare safety net be extended wider, or should it be narrowed or removed to make people more responsible for their own actions? Can one expect any reversion of values which will shift society back towards a less competitive and individualistic course, restoring at least elements of security and solidarity, or are these utopian and nostalgic fantasies? These, of course, are not new questions, but a risk society perspective may help to think about them in new ways.

Notes

1. Some material about individual changes in earnings is contained in Elias and Gregory (1994).

2. See White (1991).

3. A careful forecasting study for the USA (Leontief and Duchin, 1986) has documented the potential loss of middle-management and clerical jobs.

4. These are hitherto unpublished figures from the 'Employment in Britain' survey. For further details, see Gallie and White (1993).

5. With increasing experience and job tenure, one would have expected the general tendency to be towards increased security. In fact, this applied only to those aged under 25, who tended to feel more secure as they got themselves initially established.

6. In some cases, service contracts rather than employment contracts are used; the individuals concerned are then technically self-employed.

7. See also the following comments about self-employment, from which it is hard to disentangle work on fixed contracts.

8. See Davis (1991); BBC (1992).

9. This material is drawn from Woolf and Holly, with Varlaam (1994).

10. Performance management systems can also be related to the efficiency wage theories advanced by some economists as an explanation of high equilibrium levels of unemployment.

11. For a thorough analysis of these specific issues in the USA, see Bok (1993). In theory the high rewards for senior executives and other groups might be justified through increased productivity. Bok argues that there is no basis in evidence for suggesting that such a link exists.

12. Note that initial or transition training (e.g. for school leavers) is not included in these figures.

13. In this section, I have drawn upon material and interpretations supplied by

colleagues in ECUNET, a European network on unemployment research supported under the EC's Poverty-3 programme.

14. All consideration of the European Union is limited to the 12 countries which were members before the latest round of expansion.

15. An attraction of the 'risk society' approach is, precisely, that it stresses reasons for expecting similarities, rather than differences, in the experience of the advanced market economies.

16. This conforms roughly to the influential model of unemployment proposed by Harris and Todaro in 1970.

17. Again, substantial numbers of seasonal workers (in agriculture, construction, and more recently tourism) have been supported by special State benefits in such a way that these occupations have not become casualised.

18. This idea has been particularly applied to black families in the USA: see Ricketts (1989).

19. This is based on modelling studies in recent research at PSI, publication forthcoming.

References

BBC (1992) *Extending Choice: The BBC's Role in the New Broadcasting Age*

Beck, U. (1992) *Risk Society: Towards a New Modernity*, Sage

Bleeke, J. (1993) 'Strategic choices for newly opened markets', in J. Bleeke and D. Ernst (eds) *Collaborating to Compete*, Wiley

Bok, D. (1993) *The Cost of Talent*, Free Press

Bryson, A. and White, M. (1995) *From Unemployment to Self-employment*, Draft report to the Department of Social Security, PSI

Confederation of British Industry (1994) *Flexible Workers: Who Pays for Training?* CBI

Daniel, W. W. (1990) *The Unemployed Flow*, PSI

Davis, J. (1991) *TV, UK: A Special Report*, Knowledge Research with the Independent Programme Producers Association and The Producers Association

Elias, P. and Gregory. M. (1994) *The Changing Structure of Occupations and Earnings, 1975–1990*, Employment Department Research Series no. 27

Etzioni. A. (1975) A *Comparative Analysis of Complex Organizations*, revised and enlarged edition, Free Press

Ford, J., Kempson, E. and Wilson, M. (1995) *Mortgage Arrears and Possessions: Perspectives for Borrowers, Lenders and the Courts*, HMSO

Gallie, D. (ed.) (1994) *Processes of Detachment from the Labour Market*, Report to the European Commission, Nuffield College

Gallie, D. and White, M. (1993) *Employee Commitment and the Skills Revolution*, PSI

Gallie, D., White, M., Cheng, Y. and Tomlinson, M. (forthcoming) *Restructuring the Employment Relationship* (provisional title), in preparation

Gershuny, J. and Marsh, C. (1994) 'Unemployment in work histories', in D. Gallie, C. Marsh, and C. Vogler (eds) *Social Change and the Experience of Unemployment*, Oxford University Press

Gialloretto, M. (1988) *Strategic Airline Management: The Global War Begins*, Pitman

Government Actuary's Department (1991) *Occupational Pension Schemes 1991*, HMSO

Harris, J. and Todaro, M. (1970) 'Migration, unemployment and development: a two-sector analysis', *American Economic Review*, vol. 60

Harrison, B. and Bluestone, B. (1988) *The Great U-Turn: Corporate Restructuring and the Polarizing of America*, Basic Books

Hasluck, C. and Green, A. (1994) 'Implications of the changing spatial incidence of the long-term unemployed for the planning of programme provision and raining', in M. White (ed.) *Unemployment and Public Policy in a Changing Labour Market*, PSI

Ingram, P. N. (1991) 'Changes in working practices in British manufacturing industry during the 1980s: a study of employee concessions made during wage negotiations', *British Journal of Industrial Relations*, vol. 29

Lampard, R. (1994) 'An examination of the relationship between marital dissolution and unemployment', in D. Gallie, C. Marsh and C. Vogler (eds) *Social Change and the Experience of Unemployment*, Oxford University Press

Leontief, W. and Duchin, F. (1986) *The Future Impact of Automation on Workers*, Oxford University Press

McRae, S. (1987) *Young and Jobless*, PSI

Mendras, H. (1990) 'La force des traditions', in D. Schnapper and H. Mendras (eds) *Six manières d'être Européen*, Gallimard

Metcalf, H. (1994) 'Just a load of dossers? Homeless people and employment', in M. White (ed.) *Unemployment and Public Policy in a Changing Labour Market*, PSI

National Association of Pension Funds (1993) *Annual Survey of Occupational Pension Schemes 1992*, NAPF

Paugam, S. (1994) *Appréhension de la pauvreté sous l'angle de la disqualification sociale*, Rapport final (2 vols), Observatoire Sociologique du Changement (CNRS/FNSP)

Payne, J. and Payne, C. (1993) 'Unemployment and peripheral work', *Work, Employment and Society*, vol. 7

Pieretti, G. *et al* (1993) *Poverty and Extreme Poverty in Europe*, Report to the European Commission, University of Bologna

Reyneri, E. (1994) 'Italy: a long wait in the shelter of the family and of safeguards from the State', in O. Benoit-Guilbôt and D. Gallie (eds) *Long-Term Unemployment*, Pinter Publishers

Ricketts, E. (1989) 'The origin of black female-headed families', *Focus*, vol. 12, 1989

Storey, J. *et al* (1993) *Human Resource Management Practices in Leicestershire: A Trends Monitor*, Loughborough University Business School

Tomlinson, M. (1994) *The Persistence of Unemployment in Work Histories*, Conference paper, 1994 Work, Employment and Society Conference (mimeo), Nuffield College

Waterman, R. H., Jr., Waterman, J. A. and Collard, B. A. (1994) 'Toward a career-resilient work-force', *Harvard Business Review*, July–August

White, M. (1991) *Against Unemployment*, PSI

White, M. and Gallie, D. (1994) 'Employers' policies and individual life chances' in J. Rubery, and F. Wilkinson (eds) *Employer Strategy and the Labour Market*, Oxford University Press

White, M. and McRae, S. (1989) *Young Adults in Long-term Unemployment*, PSI

Wilkinson, F. and White, M. (1994) 'Product-market pressures and employers' responses', in J. Rubery and F. Wilkinson (eds) *Employer Strategy and the Labour Market*, Oxford University Press

Woolf, M. and Holly, S., with Varlaam, C. (1994) *Employment Patterns and Training Needs 1993/4: Freelance and Set Crafts Research*, Skillset

Disjointed interaction: the labour market and the benefits system

Andrew Shaw and Robert Walker

Introduction

Capitalist economies require most people to work. It is through employment that wealth is generated and income distributed, taxes paid and welfare systems funded. It is generally assumed that citizens need to work to become active consumers and to provide for times when they are unable to work. Many additionally gain status and satisfaction as a result of working, while a minority are exempted from the obligation to work due to age, caring responsibilities, disability, etc.

However, the advanced western economies seem increasingly to be unable to generate employment for all the people who would like to work, or to do so at wage levels that provide incomes which workers consider adequate. There are, no doubt, many reasons for this mismatch. One reason, probably not a very important one, is the subject of this chapter: work disincentives and the unsatisfactory relationship that exists between the worlds of work and benefit.

When discussing work incentives, it is helpful to distinguish between two conceptually distinct elements. Work disincentives have attracted most political attention and relate to the relative gains accruing from work and benefit. However, perhaps just as important are the barriers that the benefits system sets up which make it difficult to move from benefit into paid employment.

Reducing work disincentives has been an explicit objective of policy development for over a decade, and an implicit objective for much longer (Walker, Shaw and Hull, 1995). Nonetheless, substantial reforms have failed either to eliminate them or to ensure a comprehensive delivery of benefits to customers. Long-standing deficiencies remain, some new measures do not function well and certain changes served only to increase disincentives. Moreover, the tendency has been for social security provision to become more rigid, stringent and austere just when the 'flexible' labour market has burgeoned. As a result benefit regulations often impede or prevent, rather than enable or support, the pursuit of work opportunities. Barriers to work have increased while work disincentives remain.

This is not to say that there have been no improvements. Simply that new policies to enhance work incentives have frequently been undermined by other policy developments. Moreover, for the most part adjustments in social security provisions have addressed the supply side of the labour market at a time when developments of momentous proportions have been occurring on the demand side. It is all rather like a mechanic attempting to fine-tune an engine that is simultaneously being modified by the engineer as the aircraft continues to fly towards some uncertain destination.

The chapter divides into three. The first section is devoted to the structural features of the economy and social security system that might conspire to erode work incentives; while the second is focused on aspects of administration which though often neglected, may be both of considerable practical importance and more amenable to speedy change. The third section briefly considers strategies for reform. The reader should be warned that the analysis presented is a snapshot and therefore rather static, when in reality the labour market and policies are changing rapidly.

Finally, although the discussion focuses on work disincentives, it must be emphasised at the outset that life on income support (Britain's principal benefit for people who are out of work) is itself a major incentive to find work (Dobson *et al*, 1994; Hedges, 1993; Kempson *et al*, 1994). Living standards are generally bare and basic, with despondency and social exclusion common among recipients (Kempson *et al*, 1994). Nearly everyone wants very much to move off income support and, of course, many people do so (Ashworth and Walker, 1994; Dawes, 1993). However, finding work can be very difficult. There is no doubt that the shortage of reasonably paid, full-time jobs is the major obstacle to people moving off benefit. There are, though, several other ways in which the benefit system and labour market combine to make it particularly difficult to secure and hold down adequately rewarding work.

Structural faults

The realisation that the interaction between the structure of the benefit system and labour market might operate to lessen the effectiveness of both is not new. Indeed, it explains the creation of labour exchanges ahead of the introduction of unemployment benefit in 1911. However, it was not until 1979 that enhancing incentives, by reducing taxes for top earners and benefits for the unemployed, became a central tenet of Government policy. Ironically, as detailed elsewhere (Walker, 1994), economic change coupled with other Government policies has probably created a structure of disincentives as bad as at any time in post-war history. The pressures in the labour market that have changed the nature of work and precipitated higher levels of unemployment are undoubtedly the most important motors generating new disincentives. However, developments in policy, notably the demise of social insurance and the growth of means testing, should not be overlooked and are considered first.

The demise of social insurance

Social insurance was once the centrepiece of Britain's post-war welfare state provision for unemployed people, but is now reduced to an adjunct to means testing. Originally offering flat-rate benefits for flat-rate contributions, the scheme briefly resembled the Continental model of earnings-related contributions and benefits until the latter were abolished 15 years ago. Now only one registered unemployed claimant in five receives any unemployment benefit (Social Security Statistics, 1994) and, with the introduction of jobseeker's allowance in 1996, contribution-based entitlement will be limited to six months. It would appear that the 90-year experiment in social insurance, based on the collectivisation of risk and the right to benefit in periods of unemployment in return for contributions, is about ended.

Since the earnings-related component was abolished, unemployment benefit has retained its real value[1] although the level of benefit has fallen relative to earnings. One justification for the removal of earnings-related unemployment benefit payments in 1980 was that some people stood to be little better off in work than on benefit; that is they were subject to the so-called 'unemployment trap'. (Another rather contradictory justification was that very few recipients of unemployment benefit actually qualified for the earnings-related component.) Lowering the benefit lessened this disincentive but forced more people to rely on means-tested benefits and thereby increased the number exposed to potential disincentive effects. Indeed, work disincentives are inherent in any system that withdraws benefit as income from other sources, specifically earnings, increases, although the worst excesses can be alleviated by careful benefit design and implementation.

However, when unemployment is high and low wages are common, methods of overcoming the deficiencies often prove impractical, ineffective, hugely complicated or simply a source of new problems. Attempts to target benefits on those in most need can generate further disincentives. Take, for example, entitlement to income support, which is now conditional on neither partner in a couple working as much as 16 hours per week; this discourages people – mostly women – from maintaining half-time and/or low-paid jobs. Similarly, seeking to encourage people to save for, or to insure against, unemployment, can be counterproductive if savings or investment income count against a person's entitlement to benefit. Most self-evidently, exhortations to keep in touch with the world of work seem unconvincing when set against an earnings disregard for most unemployed people of just £5 per week.

The high unemployment of the last 15 years has meant that the proportion of unemployed people entitled to unemployment benefit has fallen steadily. At the same time, the value of means-tested support has declined relative to wages, eroding the financial protection afforded to the unemployed. This has been deliberate policy, designed to prevent people being 'trapped' in unemployment by high levels of benefit.

Trapping the unemployed

On paper it might appear that unemployed people who receive the same or more in benefit than they could earn in work will face strong employment disincentives, and therefore fall into the so-called unemployment trap (Jenkins and Millar, 1989; Millar, 1994). Economic analysis has demonstrated that these disincentives are particularly severe for specific groups of people and have measurable consequences. 'A woman married to an employed man, for example, is almost *three times* as likely to be in a job herself as a woman married to a man without a job' (Commission on Social Justice (CSJ), 1994).

However, there is a difference between the nominal existence of disincentives and the real effect that they have on claimants' behaviour. Leaving aside specific although important exceptions such as married women, the size and even the existence of disincentive effects have yet to be conclusively demonstrated (Millar, 1994; McLaughlin, 1994). Indeed, Dawes (1993), in a recent study of long-term unemployment and labour market flexibility, concluded that:

> [A]t the levels of benefit which have been considered, the commonly-held assumption that decreasing the levels of benefit (or withholding benefit) will cause an increase in flows off the unemployment register is false.

McLaughlin's (1994) assessment is more measured but has similar implications for policy. An extensive review of the effect of benefits on (un)employment led her to conclude 'that the level of unemployment benefit does have some impact on the duration of individuals' unemployment spells, but the effect is a rather small one'. Following Atkinson and Micklewright (1991) and Dilnot (1992), she states that the level of unemployment benefits in the UK could not be said to contribute to an explanation of unemployment to a degree that is useful when considering policy. Moreover, 'absolutely massive cuts' in unemployment benefit levels would be required to have any significant impact on the duration and level of unemployment. Furthermore, the effect of such cuts would be to create a regime so different from the present one from which the estimates of elasticities (of unemployment duration with respect to out-of-work benefits) are derived, that their predictive usefulness would be very suspect (Dilnot, 1992).

These findings call into question the validity of at least one of the key assumptions underlying economic analysis: namely that people will not work unless they receive more income than they can obtain on benefit. Not everybody would be prepared to do so, but many studies show that significant numbers work for benefit-level incomes, with some people actually working for less income than they could receive from out-of-work social security benefits (McKay and Marsh, 1994). Moreover, there are good rational reasons to do so. Work confers social status and improves self-esteem, and those in work tend to suffer less ill health and domestic stress. In particular, people may rightly judge that future prospects may be enhanced by being in work. In addition, as is further discussed below, some people may be working simply in ignorance of the alternatives.

There is also evidence that most unemployed people continue quite diligently to look for work while unemployed. They are also prepared to modify notions that they might have about the wage they should get, or below which they would not work (their 'reservation wage'), in the light of the actual job offers that they receive (Dawes, 1993). Indeed, there is increasing evidence that people's perceptions of the stability and security of income flows, and being able to bridge the gap between benefit and the first wage slip, are as important as the actual wage (McLaughlin, 1994).

It seems, therefore, that the lack of a positive financial incentive to work probably does not 'trap' enormous numbers of people. But there are many ways in which people can be worse off in work. Some of the more important ones are discussed below.

Work costs

In general, British social assistance has ignored the costs of working and thereby failed to ensure that people are better off in work. Where these are significant, disposable net income in work can easily dip below benefit levels.

Child care is an important and instructive example. A disregard has been available since 1994 under the family credit scheme (family credit is an in-work, income-tested benefit for families with dependent children) and other in-work benefits. Though likely to be welcomed by many claimants, the state's contribution is limited to a maximum of 70 per cent of costs of registered childminding, with a ceiling of £40 per week. Those forced to pay higher costs or to use different forms of paid care can still find themselves gaining little financial benefit from work. Furthermore, the disregard does not apply to income support claimants, which inhibits attempts by lone parents, among others, to stay in touch with the labour market through very part-time jobs. Earnings over £15 are deducted pound for pound, even if child-care costs exceed this figure.

Other work costs include travel, clothes and tools. The former can be especially prohibitive. A journey costing, say, £4 per day could exceed the net value of working and, since many unemployed people do not have cars, this is a real day-to-day expense. Under previous benefit regimes, the set-up costs of work, though not the replacement costs of tools and clothing, were recognised. The abolition of these allowances was perceived by local officials to be one of the more pernicious of the economies introduced in 1988 (Walker *et al*, 1992). Recent policy initiatives have reintroduced some support for the very long-term unemployed who find a job.

Mortgages
While home ownership is less prevalent among unemployed people than among the population as a whole, about 38 per cent of unemployed households are either home buyers or outright owners (Morgan, 1994) whose housing costs have never been comprehensively integrated into the benefit system. Indeed, as both the number of unemployed home owners and the level of their needs has risen, available support has been steadily reduced. Whereas income support recipients receive some help with their mortgage interest payments (50 per cent in the first 16 weeks, rising to 100 per cent thereafter), there is no help for mortgage holders in low-paid work. This significantly increases the break-even point at which employment begins to accrue a real rise in living standards and can create huge disincentives to both low-paid and insecure work.

These calculations changed from October 1995, since when new borrowers receive no mortgage interest payments for the first *nine* months of unemployment. Existing borrowers face two months without any support, and a further four with payments limited to 50 per cent of interest (Walker, Shaw and Hull, 1995). The Government anticipates that people will arrange private insurance to cover their mortgage payments, which may serve slightly to reduce the current disincentives for those who succeed in doing so.[2] Those who do not, or cannot, insure themselves will face a new and large *incentive* to work. Indeed, this large reduction in state provision could serve to test the theory that benefit cuts can crease work incentives. Home owners faced with no mortgage help for nine months may try even harder to find work, since anything they earn above income support (plus council tax) will help to limit the arrears which amass and thereby postpone the loss of their home. Some may seek to combine undeclared work with benefit, or others to move to rented accommodation.

However, anyone who remains on benefit sufficiently long to receive state support with their mortgage interest may find themselves trapped, and be very reluctant to leave benefit unless they can afford to pay back their mortgage arrears and find insurance against the growing prospect of a repeat spell of unemployment. At present a typical mortgage protection policy excludes those who have not had regular and continuous work for at least 12 months (Walker, Shaw and Hull, 1995).

Children or not

The fact that the level of wages is determined by market forces, rather than the intention to provide adequately for the needs of families, has long been recognised through family allowance, child benefit and, more recently, family credit. Child benefit, one of the last universal benefits, seems constantly to be at risk. It has survived to date because it mitigates the worst excesses of the unemployment trap for families moving off those means-tested benefits that include dependency additions for children (and because it has proved technically difficult to tax).

The disincentive effects of school meals, another aspect of child-care costs, have frequently been overlooked. Recipients of income support are eligible for free school meals, whereas families receiving family credit typically are not. Higher prices for school meals (reflecting the reduction in general local authority subsidies) mean that the gap between in- and out-of-work incomes for family credit recipients is further eroded and may even disappear. Similarly, schools often neglect family credit as a criterion for special financial assistance for children participating in the increasingly large number of intra- and extra-curriculum school activities for which there are now charges.

There is currently no general direct wage supplement for people without children, although low-paid workers can claim housing benefit and council tax benefit. As a result, partners in childless couples may feel themselves to be unable to accept wages as low as those taken by people with children, who can receive a wage supplement via family credit. This 'trap' will be eased under the contributory part of jobseeker's allowance, for the partners of claimants are to be allowed to work for up to 24 hours per week without affecting benefit. In addition, the Government is proposing to pilot a wage supplementation scheme for people without children.

Maintenance

In the USA a great deal of attention has been given to the role that maintenance payments might play in helping lone parents to return to work. If disregarded i the benefit system and treated as a tax allowance when in employment, maintenance can play a similar role to child benefit in providing a bedrock of financial support. In Britain maintenance is currently treated in full as income for the purposes of income support, but a £15 disregard is applied for the principal in-work, means-tested benefits. While this acts as a significant financial incentive to work (and remain in employment), it does nothing to enhance the financial welfare of lone parents on income support whose standar of living is, on average, lower than for any other socio-demographic group.

For the absent parent who is on income support, £2.35 can be deducted as a contribution towards the maintenance of his/her children. Given that this is likely to be less than the maintenance that they would have to pay if they were working, child support can act as a work disincentive for absent parents.

Poverty trap

Often confused in the lay person's mind with the unemployment trap, the poverty trap – the high marginal tax-benefit rate that occurs as benefit is withdrawn with rising income – has been the focus of much policy interest. The 1988 'Fowler Reforms' unified the structure of the major means tests and, by relating benefit entitlement to net rather than gross income, removed most circumstances where a person could actually be worse off after a pay rise. However, because the reforms were implemented on a nil-cost basis, lessening the depth of the poverty trap was only achieved by increasing its width and causing more people to face high, marginal tax-benefit rates over a larger range of potential earnings. The trap is particularly prevalent for families with children receiving family credit and housing benefit. A family which increases net earnings from one to two hundred pounds per week may gain less than £10 (Wilcox, 1994), even before the costs of earning the extra hundred are deducted. Most family credit recipients have a marginal tax rate of 80 per cent or more (McKay and Marsh, 1994).

Another factor that has contributed to the widening of the poverty trap has to do with housing policy and the shift from subsidising bricks and mortar to focusing help on low-income tenants. The rise in rents brought more people in scope. To restrict the resultant growth in housing benefit expenditure, the taper the rate at which benefit is withdrawn as income rises) has been increased. While growth in the number of housing benefit recipients has been contained as a result of these measures, the average payment has roughly doubled in the last decade, thereby significantly steepening the poverty trap for those 'lucky' enough still to receive benefit.

For many people, there may be no financial advantage in working longer and harder, and for some it could be counter productive. For example, a lone parent working full-time and paying for child care may find herself better off financially if she reduced the amount she works to coincide with school hours, thereby eliminating child-care costs. Similarly, the non-working partner in a family receiving family credit will find most of any part-time earnings deducted from benefits: this may constitute a personal unemployment trap (usually affecting the women and reinforcing traditional gender roles) embedded within a family poverty trap.

Nevertheless, despite the salience of the poverty trap there remains great doubt as to whether its existence really affects the labour supply decisions of current workers. Many people have no choice over their hours or wages and workers are not necessarily in a position to calculate their marginal tax-benefit rate (McKay and Marsh, 1994). So, high marginal deduction rates may not affect the labour supply decision of current workers. Indeed McLaughlin (1994: 34) concludes that there is 'no rigorous academic evidence' that the poverty trap is a major element in the labour supply decisions.

Labour market developments

It is developments in the labour market, some of them policy-led, which have most changed the pattern of work disincentives and, in turn, placed pressure for the reform of social security policy.

First, and foremost, has been the secular rise in unemployment which has grown from a higher point in each recession. Driving this trend has been the contraction of manufacturing, which has meant the loss of jobs that traditionally paid wages that could provide for the needs of a family without recourse to wage supplementation. In their place, with the growth of service sector employment, have been provided a mix of lower-skilled, less well-paid jobs, many of which are part-time and essentially short-term, and high-skilled, better-paid positions, of more indeterminate durability.

Partly because of these changes, the wage distribution has become markedly attenuated since the late 1970s, with the real earnings of the top tenth of male earners increasing by 50 per cent, while those of the bottom tenth were essentially static (Hills, 1995). At the same time the skills premium has increased, leaving the unskilled with little real hope of finding adequately paid work. In addition, changing aspirations, and perhaps the increased pressure of consumer-oriented society, have led to a growth in two-earner families and a polarisation between employment-rich and employment-poor households (Gregg and Wadsworth, 1994a).

These trends, combined with the natural dynamics of the labour market, mean that out-of-work families confront limited options. Most of the vacancies available at any one time are low paid, temporary and/or part-time, while full-time secure posts are usually snapped up by people already in employment (Gregg and Wadsworth, 1994b). The fall in the real value of benefits, combined with the higher skill and experience requirements to command a 'family' wage, mean that many families are trapped in unemployment or in the penumbra of intermittent jobs that surrounds it. Qualitative studies suggest that some families illicitly combine wage and benefit income, and that many more would do so if the opportunities were available or they had faith that they would not be caught (Kempson et al, 1994; Jordan et al, 1992).

While the policy debate invariably focuses on families, who have to climb the highest hurdle back into work, sight should not be lost of the single unemployed and those in households without children. These constitute the majority of unemployed claimants receiving income support and rather less is known of their circumstances. More may be content to live on low benefits or take the risk of not declaring incomes, but equally many are totally without the skills, qualifications or experience that are necessary to break into employment.

Failures to deliver

Most analyses of the impact of work incentives assume universal take-up of benefits, perfect knowledge and effective implementation. None of these is likely to apply in the real world, with quite important consequences for any consideration of the relationship between work and benefits.

Uncertainty

As noted above and elsewhere (Walker, 1995; Dobson et al, 1994; McLaughlin, 1994), successfully budgeting on a low income entails minimising risk and, consequently, uncertainty is an abhorrence. However, the movement into work entails just such uncertainty, concerning not only which benefits are available, but also the amount of entitlement and the level of take-home pay. Joint working between Benefits Agency and Employment Service offices has attempted to address these problems, conducting better-off calculations as a matter of course and providing fast, and super fast, tracks to the payment of family credit.

While these developments are welcome, they assume that systems are working well and typically exclude local authorities (responsible for the administration of housing benefit and with a highly variable reputation of efficiency). Delays in the payment of benefits are still experienced by sizeable minorities of claimants. In the case of family credit these are often due to a lack of compliance by employers, but can be exacerbated through the unintended consequences of performance targets introduced by both agencies. Similarly, errors in payment are far from unknown and are likely to increase as a result of some of the schemes designed to speed up benefit processing. The hassle generated for customers by problems of this kind, and indeed by the normal though quite complicated process of applying for benefits, can cause them to think twice about taking a job, especially if it is likely to be short-term.

Limited take-up

While the take-up of benefits continues to rise in all cases, it still falls far short of 100 per cent. The reasons for non-take-up are complicated, but lack of knowledge is a critical component (van Oorschot, 1995). While we can assume that most people are at least aware that benefits such as family credit exist, there can be far less certainty that they understand the details necessary to make an informed judgement about the financial merits of accepting a job or extending their hours. Whether people are aware of the various packages of passport benefits is doubtful, and details of earnings disregards may not be familiar to all those faced with the possibility of casual work.

Given that many of the changes to stimulate work incentives have involved subtle modification to benefit design, it is often the details that matter. It is therefore incumbent on the administration to grapple effectively with the admittedly different task of informing claimants of the options. To reach customers, benefits need continual, effective marketing.

Targeted policies

A mixture of resource constraints and the goal of targeting schemes on those who most need them inevitably mean that certain groups are excluded from potentially valuable services. Claimants, notably lone parents, who are not required to sign on as available for work are generally excluded from the counselling and training initiatives provided by the Employment Service and Training and Enterprise Councils. Similarly, many of the same services are not available to unemployed people until they have been claiming benefit for a certain length of time, nor to people looking for work but not claiming benefit.

The difficult issue is to decide whose interests should be given most weight in determining eligibility for the services or benefit on offer. The policy thrust in recent years tended to place the short-term interests of taxpayers and employers ahead of the needs of the unemployed and the longer-term requirement for an adequately skilled labour force.

Policy options

The choice of options for the 21st century has much to do with the faith placed in the ability of national governments operating in a global economy to influence either the characteristics of the labour market or the behaviour of individual workers. The emphasis in the last 15 years has been on adjusting individual behaviour by more or less subtle shifts in incentive structures. These were intended to free up the labour market, which in other respects (though in rhetoric rather more than fact) has been left to its own devices.

At the individual level, workers have increasingly been forced to engage with the flexible labour market, which poses risk, uncertainty and the likelihood of rapidly fluctuating income. The alternative is dependency on means-tested benefit, perhaps supplemented by casual earnings. Social security administration is governed by principles of audit, accuracy and accountability. Despite much effort, it remains comparatively inflexible and inhibits smooth transitions in and out of employment, and between changing portfolios of full-time and part-time jobs. At a policy level, social security has lagged behind the developments in the labour market, which have involved higher unemployment, lower entry wages and more precarious employment, but has mostly sought to facilitate further change of the same kind. The result is a pattern of disincentives and barriers that is as socially corrosive as ever.

There is no dearth of ideas for responding to these problems, spelled out by the Joseph Rowntree Foundation Inquiry into Income and Wealth (Barclay, 1995) and the Commission on Social Justice (1994) to name but two.

More of the same

The jobseeker's allowance is a development of current policy and serves as a model case study. The explicit labour market objectives are to exert downward pressure on unemployment levels, reduce the rate of growth of real wages and therefore, it is hoped, lead to a long-lasting increase in total employment.

Simultaneously the scheme aims further to simplify the benefit system, harmonise administrative systems between the Benefits Agency and the Employment Service, and provide for improved security and control of abuse.

For the unemployed person, jobseeker's allowance increases potential reliance on means testing, which, of course, adds to disincentives. However, this is offset by tighter conditions for the receipt of benefit, which is to be made conditional on the fulfilment of job search and other obligations agreed in a personally negotiated jobseeker's agreement. To the extent that the agreement is a contract imposing obligations on both parties, the obligation on the State is to provide a new framework of support with improved advice and assistance to find work. Additional elements include measures to ease the return to work and help people maintain contact with the labour market while out of a full-time job, and subsidies to employers to employ the formerly long-term unemployed.

The scheme is entirely consistent with a low-wage, comparatively low-skilled economy, in which the price of unemployment is borne principally by unemployed people. Those persons also carry the major responsibility for finding work, with the State bearing the cost of compensation for low wages. Whether the new approach proves to be more effective than its predecessors remains to be seen, and may well depend on the quality of the advice, assistance and training provided to people seeking work. The proposals do, though, introduce a new structure of incentives, some elements of which may turn out to be perverse. Older workers and people with health problems may seek other benefits. Some people may be discouraged from taking risky jobs, while others may feel coerced to take unsatisfactory ones. There may also be displacement and substitution effects as employed and unemployed people exchange places due to the pattern of incentives and sanctions.

Integration of tax and benefits

Radical schemes to merge tax and benefits have long been popular because of their apparent simplicity and miraculous ability to remove both unemployment and poverty traps (Clinton, Yates and Kang, 1994). Negative income schemes and a basic income guarantee are conceptually equivalent in economic terms but tend to emphasise different objectives, which usually means that they differ in cost. Although popular in theory, such schemes generally prove impossible to implement.

Negative income tax schemes merge the tax collection and benefit payment functions of Government, assessing benefit entitlement at the same time as calculating tax liabilities. This could reduce administration costs and, on the assumption that one agency collects tax and pays benefit, ensure high benefit take-up. One weakness is the need to pay out benefit in the short-term while assessing tax liability over a financial year. Another is the problem of devising a sensible way of reconciling tax and benefit units.

Income guarantee schemes pay an unconditional benefit to all citizens, financed by abolishing tax allowances. They are probably easier to administer than negative income tax schemes, but tend to be more expensive. To reduce costs, and the high marginal rates of tax this generates, some form of partial scheme is often proposed, leaving some benefits as they are. This tends to complicate administration and reintroduce the possibility of poverty traps, undermining the attractiveness of the scheme.

History shows that even reforming small parts of the social security system can present major administrative difficulties. In the light of this experience it is not self-evident that the simultaneous reform of the entire tax and benefit system is a risk worth taking, merely to remove work disincentives that two decades of research suggest are really of little consequence in themselves.

Return to social insurance
The fact that all other European Union countries persist with social insurance-based unemployment schemes may convince some commentators that social insurance is not an idea that should be pursued. Certainly there is some move away from comprehensive social insurance in several European countries and a growing reliance on means testing, predominantly as a cost-saving measure (van Oorschot, 1995). Nevertheless, social insurance has many attractions that make it appealing to others. It can enhance social cohesion, eliminate poverty traps and enable precise control to be exerted over the extent of the unemployment trap by the level at which earnings replacement is set.

Frank Field (1995) proposes a National Insurance Corporation, independent of Government, to run state insurance schemes including unemployment benefit. Payments above a basic minimum would be related to contributions and part-time workers would be covered. Recipients could then legitimately top up their incomes with part-time work or other income without fear. The comparatively small number of people claiming tax-financed income support would receive a minimal payment, conditional upon drawing up a career plan.

The Social Justice Commission also favours an enhanced unemployment benefit scheme, available to self-employed as well as employees and with a part-time component. The Commission's principal model envisages benefit being based on a minimum period of contributions, rather than a detailed contribution record, although long-term contributors could receive benefit for more than the basic 12 months. Whether the benefit would be earnings-related is unclear. The Commission also toys with the idea of a contingency-based scheme, related to an individual's current availability for work rather than based on their contribution record.

The precise impact of any of these schemes naturally depends on the institutional environment in which they are embedded and particularly the support available to meet housing costs.

Modernising means testing

Strategies of this kind would have the collective objective of making the administration of benefits more speedy, flexible and, hence, more responsive to people's needs and the requirements of a flexible labour market.

Claimants crave a simple, accessible system, which enables them to know where they stand and which provides them with accurate, adequate benefits with the minimum of hassle. (Most would also prefer jobs rather than benefits, but that requires other strategies.) Certain of the measures to be introduced in the context of jobseeker's allowance must be viewed as positive developments in an appropriate direction. An end to the need to traipse between Benefits Agency offices and Jobcentres could significantly reduce hassle for claimants, although this advance may be squandered if the combined service comes to be identified solely with the policing of job search. Provisions to extend payment of housing benefit could help many people to bridge the period of financial insecurity that often accompanies a return to work. The back to work bonus may help at a similar time and possibly serve to encourage people to maintain contact with work when they are primarily unemployed.

Other planned developments are also relevant. Fast-track systems of family credit, which involve taking claims by telephone, paying benefit and seeking definitive evidence afterwards, will also help the transition to work unless recovery of overpayments comes to dominate procedures. If 'One Stop' procedures can be made to work, and coherent advice and action are available on the spot, this should also enable people to make better informed labour market decisions. However, jobseekers might also welcome agreements that were binding on other parties: comprehensive in-work benefit calculations binding on employers and the State, and a 'no worse off in work guarantee' that helped support living standards rather than asking low-income families to forgo them.

Social assistance could be modernised in other respects to reflect current patterns of living more accurately. This might involve allowing people explicitly to create packages of income from different sources, including part-time employment and benefit. Similarly, abolishing the concept of adult dependants and moving towards individual assessment could provide additional opportunities for partners to share the role of breadwinner.

Finally, investment in information technology could be tailored more directly to the perceived needs of claimants. They would welcome any procedure that cut short the application process: being asked to update a printout of information held on file, rather than completing new forms, would be a major bonus. Some might even welcome the remodelling of social security into a social bank, with individual accounts accessible by means of plastic cards, facilities for loans and independent financial advice.

Reform of the labour market

Perhaps the majority view outside Government circles is that the confused relationships between social security and work can only be tackled by policies that involve some reform of the labour market. This is not to deny the need for a flexible labour market, rather to recognise that there is also a requirement for additional, preferably secure, employment, paying wages that can support an adequate standard of living. While all the major political parties publicly subscribe to a high-wage, high-skill economy, achieving this requires a substantial financial investment in Britain's infrastructure and workforce.

This is not the place to detail the recommendations of the Joseph Rowntree Foundation Inquiry into Income or Wealth or the Commission on Social Justice. However, it is important to recognise that both groups of experts broke with the ideology of the last decade that has declared Government impotent to affect the workings of the labour market. Instead, they advocate an approach which involves strong, positive action to:

- improve education and training

- increase labour demand

- improve the incomes of low-wage earners

- enhance the role of social insurance with improved benefit levels

- ease the transitions between benefits and paid work.

This is not to say that the task ahead is easy, nor that Government is the sole player. However, nor should obligations be placed only on job-seekers. Their responsibilities need to be matched by those of employers who must recognise the long-term consequences of their employment, training and investment decisions, and pay their share of the costs of maintaining a flexible labour market. Similarly, governments need to follow policies that equip people with the skills required to succeed in employment – to help ensure, even by direct investment, that fulfilling employment is available to all, and that workers are adequately compensated when the cost of an efficient labour market takes the form of transitory unemployment.

The obligation on taxpayers that follows from the above strategy is that they help fund investment in the infrastructure and labour market, and share the cost of international economic competition more equally with the unemployed than they do at present. The obligation on politicians is that they take the risk that taxpayers-cum-voters will abide by their side of the bargain.

Notes

1. This ignores the removal of child additions for unemployed claimants with children.

2. The limitations of existing insurance policies are discussed in Walker, Shaw and Hull (1995).

References

Ashworth, K. and Walker, R. (1994) 'Measuring claimant populations', in N. Buck, J. Gershuny, D. Rose and J. Scott (eds) *Changing Households*, ESRC/RCMC

Atkinson, A. and Micklewright, J. (1991) 'Unemployment compensation and labour market transitions: a critical review', *Journal of Economic Literature*, vol. 29, pp. 1679–727

Barclay, P. (1995) *Joseph Rowntree Foundation Inquiry into Income and Wealth*, vol. 1, Joseph Rowntree Foundation

Clinton, D., Yates, M. and Kang, D. (1994) *Integrating Taxes and Benefits?* IPPR

CSJ (1994) *Social Justice: Strategies for National Renewal*, The Report of the Commission on Social Justice, Vintage

Dawes, L. (1993) *Long-term Unemployment and Labour Market Flexibility*, Centre for Labour Market Studies, Leicester

Dilnot, A. (1992) 'Social security and labour market policy', in E. McLaughlin (ed.) *Understanding Employment*, Routledge, London

Dobson, B., Beardsworth, A., Keil, T. and Walker, R. (1994) *Diet, Choice and Poverty*, Family Policy Studies Centre

Field, F. (1995) *Making Welfare Work*, Institute of Community Studies

Gregg, P. and Wadsworth, J. (1994a) *More Work in Fewer Households?* National Institute for Economic and Social Research, Discussion Paper 72

Gregg, P. and Wadsworth, J. (1994b) *Opportunity Knocks? Job Separations, Engagements and Claimant Status*, National Institute of Economic and Social Research

Hedges, A. (1993) *In-Work Benefit Project*, DSS, Social Research Branch

Hills, J. (1995) *Joseph Rowntree Foundation Inquiry into Income and Wealth*, vol. 2, Joseph Rowntree Foundation

Hutton, W. (1995) 'Why means-testing short-changes us all', *Guardian*

Jenkins, S. and Millar, J. (1989) 'Income risk and income maintenance: implications for incentives to work', in A. W. Dilnot and I. Walker (eds) *The Economics of Social Security*, Oxford University Press

Jordan, B., James, S., Kay, H. and Redley, M. (1992) *Trapped in Poverty? Labour Market Decisions and Low Income Households*, Routledge

Jordan, B. and Redley, M. (1994) 'Polarisation, underclass and the welfare state', *Work, Employment and Society*, vol. 8, no. 2, pp. 153–76

Kempson, E., Bryson, A. and Rowlingson, K. (1994a) *Hard Times?* Policy Studies Institute

Kempson, E., Bryson, A. and Rowlingson, K. (1994b) *Struggling to Make Ends Meet*, Policy Studies Institute

McKay, S. and Marsh, A. (1994) *Lone Parents and Work*, HMSO

McLaughlin, E. (1994) *Flexibility in Work and Benefits*, Institute of Public Policy Research

Millar, J. (1994) in A. Bryson and S. McKay (eds) *Is It Worth Working?* Policy Studies Institute, London

Morgan, C. (1994) *Family Resources Survey Statistics, 1993/94*, Government Statistical Series

Morris, L. (1992) 'The social segregation of the long-term unemployed in Hartlepool', in *The Sociological Review*, 38

Oorschot, W. van (1995) *Realizing Rights*, Avebury

Payne, J. and Payne, C. (1994) 'Recession, restructuring and the fate of the unemployed', *Sociology*, vol. 28, no. 1

Walker, R. (1994) 'Springing the poverty trap?' *New Economics*, Autumn

Walker, R. (1995) 'Routes into and out of poverty over the life course', in R. Bayley, A. Condy and C. Roberts (eds) *Policies for Families: Work, Poverty and Resources*, Family Policy Study Centre

Walker, R., Dix, G. and Huby, M. (1992) *Working the Social Fund*, HMSO

Walker, R., Shaw, A. and Hull, L. (1995) 'Responding to the risk of unemployment', in *Risk, Insurance and Welfare*, Association of British Insurers

Wilcox, S. (1994) *Housing Benefit and the Disincentive to Work, Housing Policy and Economic Recovery*, Briefing Paper 4, Joseph Rowntree Foundation

6 Education, training and employment prospects

Ewart Keep and Ken Mayhew

Introduction

This chapter explores how vocational education and training (VET) can improve employment prospects. In order to answer this question we need to evaluate the contribution that VET is presently making. First, therefore, the chapter describes what have conventionally been thought to be the UK's deficiencies in VET and what has been achieved in recent years. Second it considers some major issues confronting the future of employment. Finally it reviews the implications for policy towards education and training.

British training performance

By the beginning of the 1980s there was widespread concern about Britain's poor VET performance relative to that of most of our major competitors. There was general agreement – though sometimes surprisingly little evidence – about the dimensions of these shortcomings. Too few people stayed in full-time education beyond compulsory school leaving age. Too many of those who left school at the age of 16 were lacking in numeracy and literacy. Too few went into jobs that provided real training. Those who did entered apprenticeship schemes that were often too narrow in focus and too long. Apprentices 'graduated' by serving their time, rather than by undergoing proper testing of competencies and by acquiring qualifications. There was little adult training or retraining.

The last 15 years have witnessed immense Government activity designed to address these problems. The Industrial Training Boards were abolished and with them old-style apprenticeship schemes and any real forum for co-ordination of training activities at the national level. Their demise, with that of the Manpower Services Commission, also meant the effective end of tripartite policy making and delivery. Instead, with the creation of Training and Enterprise Councils (TECs), delivery was localised and put essentially in the hands of employers. The Government stressed the desirability of testing and the achievement of qualifications. The introduction of NVQs at their various levels provided a set of such qualifications that were also meant to give a degree of comparability across industries and trades. Government money was provided through a whole succession of schemes. By the end of the decade the two dominant ones were

Youth Training (YT) and, for adults, Employment Training (ET). Subsequently YT was replaced by Training Credits and Modern Apprenticeships; Employment Training and Employment Action were replaced by Training for Work and Jobplan Workshops.

Meanwhile the education sector saw equally substantial change, increasing in pace towards the end of the decade. One important theme of this change was an avowed intent to make what the educational sector offered more relevant to the world of work. A signal of this intent was the introduction of GNVQs in vocational subjects, which were meant to achieve parity of esteem with their more academic counterparts – GCSEs and A levels.

On many conventional indicators there has clearly been an improvement in VET performance. Employers are spending more money on training and more people are recorded as undergoing training. More youths are remaining in school or other full-time education beyond the age of 16 and more are entering higher education. A greater proportion of the labour force possesses qualifications of some sort.[1] There is a limited amount of micro-evidence that we have made up some of the gap between ourselves and competitor countries.[2]

Although some commentators believe that this represents a skills revolution,[3] the general opinion among independent experts is that there are still many problems and that the UK remains, at least to an extent, the sick man of the OECD. The sceptics argue as follows. There has indeed been an increase in training activity, but much of it is of low quality. YT came to be generally regarded as mainly a subsidy to remove unemployed workers from the register. Although some YT schemes involved excellent training packages, these were in a small minority (Keep, 1994). Even by 1993/94 only 42 per cent of YT trainees were receiving an NVQ of any sort. ET had even less training content. NVQs are viewed by many with suspicion (Prais, 1989 and 1991; Smithers, 1993). NVQ 5 is meant to be the equivalent of a postgraduate degree, NVQ 4 the equivalent of an undergraduate degree, NVQ 3 of A levels and NVQ 2 of GCSEs. NVQ 1 would not be recognised as a qualification in most Continental European countries. Only 6 per cent of employers are using NVQs. Most of them are being awarded at levels 1 and 2. Industry lead bodies devise the content/syllabuses of the NVQs to be awarded in their industries. Some doubt has been voiced about the standards applied. For example, an NVQ Level 3 in fencing construction rather tests the imagination. It is still unclear precisely how adequate the testing system really is. Looking at the content of training within companies, much of it is concerned with 'social' skills or relatively low-grade IT skills. Another worrying indicator of quality is the short length of many training courses.

The output of the full-time education system is the subject of even more heated controversy. Undeniably, fewer people every year are leaving school without some form of qualification, while ever more are obtaining degrees. Yet there are potentially contra-indicators. Complaints from employers about standards of literacy and numeracy are still frequent and vociferous. A top grade at GCSE is easier to obtain than a top grade at O level, though what is perhaps more revealing is that a minimum passing grade at GCSE is *not* easier to obtain than a minimum passing grade at CSE. Few people deny that the content of A level syllabuses has been and is being thinned down. There is more dispute about whether the standards required within the restricted syllabuses are any less demanding. A reasonable preliminary conclusion would be that there has been some improvement as far as the bottom half of the ability range is concerned. The questions are how extensive this improvement has been and how far down the bottom 50 per cent it extends. Also a key issue is how far this has been at the expense of the attainment standards of the top 50 per cent. Here we must make the difficult distinction between, on the one hand, knowledge acquired and, on the other, more general intellectual skills like the ability to synthesise and analyse and, critically, the ability to learn more in the future. It is one thing for universities to receive students from the schools with less knowledge, it is quite another to receive students whose cognitive abilities are significantly less well developed. There are many unresolved issues here, but it would not be unfair to conclude that there is cause for concern.

A diagnosis of the UK's training problem

To put it mildly, the evidence is conflicting. To make more sense of it we need to diagnose the nature of Britain's training problem. There are two ways of delivering an effective VET performance. The first is the employer-based route. The second is the full-time education route. Different countries have used different mixes of these routes to good effect. Traditionally Britain has relied very heavily on the employer-based route. Here we will consider the problems experienced in employing this strategy. Later we will ask whether the full-time education route could be used to better effect.

Conventional analysis would stress an externality problem. The problem is that the return for the investment in education and training does not necessarily accrue to whoever bears the cost. Human capital theory tells us that an employer will be willing to pay for specific training (leading to skills which can be used only by the employer with whom they are acquired), but will *not* be willing to pay for general training (leading to skills which can be used by other employers). The reason for this is that an employer can recoup training costs nly by subsequently paying the worker less than the value of his/her output marginal product) which, of course, has been enhanced by the injection of raining. In the case of general training the individual's potential output has een enhanced in a way which is transferable between different working nvironments, and other employers who have not paid for the training can fford to pay the worker the full value of his/her output.

ince the employee is the one who benefits from the training, at first sight it vould appear that he or she ought to contribute to its cost. However, imperfect apital markets, imperfect information and risk aversion, among other factors, mit the extent to which he or she will do so. In the absence of the willingness of ndividual workers to take on the cost, we are in a situation where a socially ub-optimal amount of training is provided. In other words, the net returns to he economy as a whole from investment in training are greater than the erceived returns to the person or organisation who has to pay for it.

Ve know that employers do pay for some general training. As Margaret Stevens 1994) has shown in analysing what she calls transferable skills, this is not urprising. The arguments above assume that markets are in effect perfectly ompetitive. Once one allows for a variety of imperfections, then worker nobility will be restricted and poaching will be limited. However, the direction f argumentation used in the preceding paragraph remains valid, and an xternality problem of sorts will be present. There is some controversy about ow great the externality problem is.[4] It is a difficult debate to resolve, since by he nature of the issue it is difficult to obtain hard evidence. Our own inclination s to believe that externalities are significant, but remember that there is nothing eculiarly British about externalities. Any particular difficulties they pose for the JK would be the consequence of our failure to deal with them as effectively as ther countries. However, we believe that there is a second, more deep-seated nhibitor of training performance – the lack of employer demand for skills.

'here are several reasons why we suspect that there is weak employer demand or skill. Many employers were publicly sceptical of the feasibility of the lifelong earning targets set by the National Education and Training Targets (see Keep nd Mayhew, 1994a). Although skill differentials appear to have widened in ecent years, the work of, among others, Bennett et al (1992) suggests that the ate of return to individuals from lower-level qualifications is still modest. In ther words, employers are often reluctant to reward skill with additional pay. 'he importance of formal skills in the selection process is reported to be low. As ve have already argued, the skill content of the NVQs employers have devised ; often flimsy by European standards. The failure of employers to provide sustained and high-quality training was one reason for the failure of YT.

Some[5] cite evidence that they believe shows there is not a low demand for skills. We are inclined not to weight their evidence very strongly. Skill-shortage surveys report the difficulties that employers experience in recruiting staff who are already trained; but, among the reasons for their difficulties, are inadequate pay and a reluctance to train their existing staff. Gallie and White (1993) suggest that higher qualification levels demanded by employers provide evidence of rising demand for skills. Yet employers might simply be using qualifications as screening devices, with the screen becoming tougher in response to rising educational qualifications. By itself such evidence does not necessarily mean that employers are using their more-qualified recruits any more productively than the less-qualified ones of a few years back.

Why is there weak demand for skills? One factor is the inherited tradition of industrial relations in Britain. This tradition was confrontational and involved a deep-seated 'them and us' attitude among management. There was an evident belief that firms were best staffed by a smallish elite of the skilled and technically competent and a large group of workers who were discouraged from thinking for themselves, being expected to do what they were told. Though one declared aim of human resource management (HRM) techniques is to remedy this attitude, the overwhelming volume of empirical evidence suggests that only a few companies have actually taken up a full-blown sophisticated HRM model.

In most companies a coherent approach has been lacking. Worse than that, as the old collective bargaining model of employee relations has declined, it has not been replaced by any considered strategy of employee involvement. Millward (1994) has commented that in many British companies workers are treated simply like a commodity or a factor of production. Sisson argued that 'for the average UK employee the experience of personnel management in Britain in the mid-1990s is less like the "HRM organisation" than it was a decade ago' (1994: 41). But unless companies have the personnel management systems that can capture the motivational benefits of training, and of creating forms of job design and work organisation that can provide opportunities for greater worker autonomy and the utilisation of higher levels of skill, demand for skills will be limited and the utilisation of existing skills inefficient.

Short-termism has become almost a catch-phrase, but serious issues still need investigation. If short-termism exists then it will militate against investment of all types, including investment in training. Whether the City imposes short-termism on the rest of the economy is still a matter of dispute.[6] What is clear is

1at companies' own organisational control mechanisms often impose similar
onstraints. Although there are some early signs of reaction to decentralised and
evolved decision taking, until recently the fashion has been for the devolution
f responsibility and authority. To an extent this was inevitable in multi-product,
onglomerate companies, but the fashion was not confined to them, being
vident also in single-product companies. A smallish corporate HQ supervised
1e activities of semi-autonomous divisions, cost centres or profit centres. A key
ecision which the HQ had to make was how to allocate scarce financial
esources to each of these units. A number of writers have described the
nancial portfolio management techniques used to make such decisions.
ssentially this involved awarding resources based on recent below-the-line
erformance. Thus there was limited incentive for the managers of these
evolved units to adopt policies that had anything other than a short-term
ay-off.

Vhy should such techniques have been used? In part it has been attributed to
1e dominance of the finance and accounting function among top management
1 Britain, and in part to the difficulties (through lack of expertise) of applying
1ore complex criteria when judging the relative success of quasi-autonomous
usinesses, often producing very different goods or services and often operating
1 very different markets. It has led to a control system which has been describ-
d by Goold and Campbell (1986) as 'peering at business through numbers'.
'erhaps linked with this, managerial rewards and promotions tend to be related
ery strongly to short-term performance.

 more extreme variant of the argument about lack of employer demand for
kill is intimately linked to corporate product strategy. This is the low-skills,
ow-quality equilibrium hypothesis, associated with Finegold and Soskice
1988). An example will illustrate the ideas behind the hypothesis. Imagine that
t some point in the past a company has found it difficult to recruit sufficient
killed workers. It makes do by devices such as relaxing hiring standards or
educing recruitment requirements. This may lead it to modify the production
rocess. As a result of this the company finds itself producing relatively low-
pecification products. It may become very good at this and it might take very
1rge shocks or extreme changes in incentives to persuade the company to alter
trategy and start producing at the high-specification end of the product range.
raditional assembly line or 'Fordist' production arrangements are associated
vith low-specification products. Much the same thing is produced year after
ear. Thus production engineers can devise processes which rely on long and
epeated runs and achieve significant economies of scale. Meanwhile work
tudy engineers can segment tasks in such a way as to create 'simple', repetitive

jobs for which little skill or adaptability is required. The implication for the demand for skills is obvious. Competition is by cost per unit of output.

By contrast, a high-specification product strategy involves incorporating many characteristics in the good being produced, and involves changing these characteristics frequently to meet ever-changing consumer tastes and needs. The associated production strategy is often described as post-Fordist. Long production runs are impossible to achieve, and by definition economies of scale are harder to obtain. Remaining competitive now depends on the specification itself and on keeping ahead of the market. Cost is not unimportant, but it is less dominating in a company's competitive strategy. Jobs cannot so easily be broken down into simple repetitive tasks. There simply is not time for that. Rather, at all levels the workforce has to be capable of meeting change, and be adaptable, self-reliant and more able to learn on the job – in the process contributing to the fine-tuning of the productive process. In such circumstances the demand for skill in the broadest sense of the word is undoubted. Advocates of the low-quality, low-skills hypothesis contend that too many British companies have chosen the low-specification route.

Clinching evidence on the hypothesis is hard to find. But there is some. The work done by Sig Prais and his colleagues at the National Institute,[7] comparing the production of a whole range of goods and services in Britain and other countries (usually Germany), has found a number of cases where specification appears to be lower than in the comparator country. Nick Oulton's (1995) evidence that the UK appears to have a low volume of high-unit-value exports points in the same direction, as does the more general study of UK trade performance by Buxton *et al* (1994).

Much of the research has been done on manufacturing. An interesting, but as yet unresolved, question is how far similar analysis can be applied to services. Certainly we can observe Fordist strategies being applied to some areas of service activity, not least in clearing banking and retailing. Many of the organisations employing such strategies would argue that, unlike manufacturing, it is consistent with delivering at the high-specification end of their markets. This is an issue which requires further investigation.

The prospects for employment

The brief of this chapter is to explore what VET can do to improve employment prospects in the UK. This can be considered at a number of levels. The obvious question is how the prospects of the unemployed can be helped by training.

There is a more general, but equally important question. This is how employment prospects for a much larger segment of the labour force can be improved. Authors like Soskice (1993) think of the workforce as comprising an upper third for whom the prospects are and remain rosy, a bottom third where the prospects are awful – facing unemployment, low labour force attachment, and low pay. The critical question is what happens to the middle third. Are they likely to be relatively low skilled and low paid because their employers survive by cost competition? Or will they be more highly skilled and paid?

The background to this question is provided by the well-known projections of a changing structure of employment which are set out in Chapter 2. These projections suggest that part-time jobs will represent an ever bigger slice of work, the proportion of women in the labour force will continue to grow, and small firms will be the biggest generators of jobs. Traditionally part-timers and workers in smaller firms have been relatively badly trained. The picture for women is more complex, but certainly large sub-groups of them appear to have suffered in the training stakes. Employment is expected to fall in the primary industries, construction, manufacturing, the utilities, distribution and transport. It is expected to grow in private and public services. Accompanying this changing industrial composition, unskilled manual occupations are projected to decline in significance, as are well paid semi-skilled and skilled manufacturing jobs. Conversely there will be more professional and managerial jobs. While there will be an occupational upgrading of the labour force, the projections also suggest a substantial growth in some traditionally low-paid areas such as sales and security.

In brief, the projections are consistent with the possibility that substantial segments of the workforce could remain or become relatively disadvantaged, against a backcloth of a workforce which on average is improving on conventional measures of occupational status. What can VET policy do to improve prospects for the unemployed and more generally for the middle third?

VET and the unemployed

We first consider what can be done for the unemployed. First it is necessary to outline the schemes currently available. Youth Training is due to be replaced by Training Credits in 1996. Credits are a form of voucher by which a young person can pay for further education or training. The Modern Apprenticeship Scheme will re-route at least some of the funds to training for youths other than those who would otherwise have been unemployed. We have already suggested that while YT increased the volume of training available to the young unemployed, little of it was of high quality. A necessarily preliminary judgement on Training Credits would be similar. Modern Apprenticeships might be regarded as the last throw for employer-based training. The Government clearly sees them as an attempt to redress the balance of quality against quantity. If the scheme fails it is difficult to see what else can be done via official schemes. ET has been even more widely acknowledged as a failure as far as training content was concerned.

As noted above, Employment Training (ET) and Employment Action (EA) have already been replaced by Training for Work and Jobplan Workshops. In 1993 Community Action and Workstart were introduced. The 1993 Budget also introduced Learning for Work. The consensus is that the training content of this battery of measures for adults is limited.

In considering what more can done, three general points need to be noted. First, there is a limit to the extent to which training can manufacture job creation for the unemployed. Second, there will remain many jobs for which skill requirements are low. Training in the strictest sense of the word will be of limited use here. Third, older workers are likely to experience continuing difficulties, stemming not so much from their lack of skills and capabilities, but from the prevailing climate of thinking about their role in organisations. Nevertheless even with level funding more could be done. An important pre-condition is that policy makers have to realise how resistant many disadvantaged workers are to training. This resistance can be overcome only by clear and demonstrable links between training programmes and future economic welfare.

The following are our suggestions.

- The experience of ET, and to a lesser extent of YT, suggests that it might be better to provide a smaller number of better-funded training places – that is to prefer quality to quantity.

- Funding arrangements must avoid pushing trainees towards lower-level skills and discriminating against those most in need of help. This has often been the implication of incentive regimes driven by outcome-related funding with which the TECs have been faced.

- Even more needs to be done to improve the initial education of the low achievers. Future labour market prospects are heavily dependent on what is achieved at school.

- The experience of REPLAN suggests that much is to be gained from offering educational opportunities to the adult unemployed. REPLAN had a significant effect on the many further education colleges. It provided not only vocational courses but was also concerned to develop personal and social skills. The FE colleges were encouraged to experiment with new curricula and delivery mechanisms and to improve contacts with local communities.

- More needs to be done to ensure life-long learning and continued training and development for those in employment. Prevention is better than cure.

- More integration is needed between VET measures and other initiatives, in areas such as community education, job creation, small business start-up schemes and community enterprise.

- Currently the TECs have the prime responsibility for delivering training for the unemployed. Many of them have exhibited a distinct lack of enthusiasm for this role, which some commentators claim has distracted them from the task of upgrading the skills of the employed. Perhaps more of the training for the unemployed should be handed over to local authorities, voluntary organisations and educational establishments.

- Given the relative failure of more conventional schemes, perhaps a more radical alternative is called for. In the US there has been much debate about a national service programme. Something of a similar nature is worth investigating in the UK, though we do not underestimate the difficulties and problems that such a scheme would have to surmount (Gardiner, 1995).

There have been some pleasing developments, which indicate a move away from a simple reliance on mass participation low-level training schemes towards broader measures encompassing adult education (Learning for Work), work experience (Community Action) and job subsidies (Workstart). But much remains to be done. Policy makers need to distinguish more clearly between those who can most benefit from skill acquisition, those who can most benefit from a rebuilding of suitable and positive attitudes towards work, and those for whom perhaps the best solution is to become self-employed.

Employment prospects and VET

We now move on to discuss more general aspects of the UK's employment prospects. The starting point is our earlier proposition that the demand for skills is weak. Why should we worry about this? The answer relates to what happens to the middle third of the labour force. If we are correct in our contention that the low demand for skills is intimately linked to product strategy, then the implications for this middle third are disturbing. By definition, competition in such products is cost competition. In this day and age low-specification products are produced not only by other developed economies, but also in many Third World countries. Access to the appropriate technology and to the capabilities to utilise it is now relatively easy. This means that such countries can achieve at least similar productivity levels as Western countries producing similar commodities. Transport costs and taste differences sometimes limit the extent of competition from this source. Nevertheless if UK firms are to survive in these markets, in the medium term their labour costs broadly defined must be on a par with those of the relevant Third World competitors. Across a range of products, the Third World will force cost competition upon us if our products are low specification. But even where such external competition is not at issue, it is also a matter of how our own companies choose to position themselves; and this applies as much to services (retailing and banking, for example) as to manufacturing. The deregulation of the 1980s in many senses makes it more attractive than otherwise for UK employers to follow the low-specification route. The implications for pay and for rights at work are obvious.

Considerations such as these are behind the contrast which has recently been drawn between the labour market experiences of the US, on the one hand, and of Continental Europe on the other. Over the last two decades the US has experienced a smaller rise in unemployment and a greater rise in inequality. It has appeared to some commentators that this is a matter of 'you pay your money and you take your choice'. If the wages of less-skilled labour are not downwardly flexible then jobs will not be available. Without questioning the general proposition that labour market flexibility of this kind can enhance employment prospects, Richard Freeman (1995) has questioned whether in this specific instance it has been employment generating for the US.

Clearly the issue of the relationship between wage flexibility and unemployment involves many issues other than how to meet the threat of Third World competition. However, this is one important element and has been systematically discussed by Adrian Wood (1994), among others. Using a traditional analytical framework known as the Heckscher-Ohlin model as his starting point, he argues that the Third World would tend to specialise in products which use relatively intensively that factor in which it is abundant – less-skilled labour. By contrast, developed countries will specialise in those products which use relatively intensively skilled labour. The implication is that if employment of less-skilled

bour is to be maintained in developed economies then its relative price has
fall. Nickell and Bond (1995) have investigated how much of the rise in
nemployment in the UK is a consequence of 'biased' demand shifts against
he unskilled, and conclude that it accounts for 20 per cent of the rise in
nemployment. However, their estimates are heavily reliant on a variety of
ssumptions used.

t the very least, the current debate shows that unskilled labour has been
aving a tough time and things are likely to get tougher. It suggests very
trongly to us that it is important for policy makers to turn their attention to
olicies designed to boost the demand for skills, and that such policies cannot be
ivorced from corporate product strategies. We suggested some avenues in an
arlier paper (Keep and Mayhew, 1994a) and we summarise them below.

A common view of society. This involves achieving some consensus about
the sort of society in which we wish to live. The Government seems to
envisage a high-skill society, but this is not accompanied by any real
appreciation that anything needs to be done to foster a high-specification
product strategy. Rather the assumption is that this will emerge through
the operation of market forces. Our analysis suggests that this cannot be
relied upon. Other countries which pride themselves on competition and
the successful harnessing of market forces just as much as ours seem to
have no intellectual difficulty in combining this with industrial strategies
in various guises which foster a high-specification product strategy. Worse
still, this official vision of a high-skill society is accompanied by policies
which might be thought to encourage many British employers in their
pursuit of a low-skill, low-pay, low-specification strategy.

The above almost certainly implies that a new and more participative
model of VET policy making is needed. Without some agreement that high
product specification is what is being aimed for, then trainers and the
training industry lack a contextual framework within which to direct their
efforts.

If such a framework were present, then a variety of levers are available.
Tax-based incentives and penalties would be worth considering. So might
direct legislative intervention and improved help and advice to
particularly small businesses. Without the framework, such approaches
are likely to be at best futile and at worst lead to wasteful expenditure,
whether by Government or by industry.

- Supply chain pressures might prove to be helpful, but again these would lead into a virtuous circle only if sufficient firms were producing high-specification products.

- Various sections of the Labour Party have argued that one justification of the minimum wage would be that the requirement on employers to pay higher wages would force them to adopt a higher-skill and higher-specification product strategy. Given the complexity of the systems failure we have described, this is almost certainly over-optimistic.

- An important lever might be the creation of a more secure labour market environment. Both numerical and functional flexibility have produced some positive results . But there have also been costs. The emergence of a core/periphery strategy carries with it the danger that employers abandon responsibility to provide training for a large proportion of their employees. We need to consider whether flexibility can be retained without this consequence.

- Personnel management systems in many organisations would need to be substantially upgraded, and their links with wider business strategy greatly strengthened.

None of these are easy solutions, and all would require a radically different view of policy and policy making to stand any chance of being implemented successfully. Moreover, it is important to recognise that there are no quick or simple solutions to what we perceive to be a complex systems failure. One radical alternative to the type of policy thrust we have been suggesting has been proposed by David Soskice (1993), among others. He suggests that the employer-based approach has failed, stressing many of the arguments that we have made about the lack of demand for skill. However, there has been a dramatic increase in participation in full-time education. Much of this increased participation may have occurred for negative reasons – reaction to the recession. However, he argues, why not harness these developments?

The low-skills, low-quality equilibrium may be a difficult one from which to escape, but it is not impossible. The product strategy an employer uses is in the end a matter of cost-benefit considerations, and if the incentives are sufficiently strong then he or she may well make the switch of strategy. If a supply of skilled labour is readily available this would act as such an incentive, as would the aspirations of this more highly qualified workforce. It is possible, but by no means certain. We have many examples from the past of occupational filtering down – the phenomenon of jobs previously being done by, for example, non-graduates now being done by graduates. But this has not necessarily led to them being done any better, or to a transformation of the product or service being offered by their employers. If filtering down occurs, then there is potential for massively wasted social expenditure.

If nothing else, this chapter indicates the complexity of the problems that confront policy makers, not least those in the newly unified Department for Education and Employment. The great danger is that, faced with these difficulties, politicians will resort to yet more incremental tinkering with the institutional mechanisms of skill supply, and leave nearly all else to 'the market'. To date, such an approach has not solved the underlying weaknesses in Britain's skills base, and we would argue that it is unlikely to prove any more effective in the future. Problems with a weak demand for skills call for a different type of response. Moreover, a more integrated approach to the relationships that exist between, on the one hand, vocational education and training policies and, on the other, wider structural developments in the labour market, is in our view a prerequisite for sustained progress.

Notes

1. These trends can be discerned by examining successive issues of the Employment Department's annual *Training Statistics*.

2. See, for example, Hawkins and Steedman (1993).

3. See, for example, Gallie and White (1993).

4. Among the authorities who put some emphasis on the 'poaching' problem were the CBI (1989: 33) and Morris *et al* (1991). However, the influential *Challenge to Complacency* (Coopers and Lybrand, 1985: 11) was inclined to lay less stress on poaching.

5. See, for example, Gallie and White (1993).

6. See, for example, Marsh (1990).

7. See, for example, Prais (1990).

References

Bennett, R., Glennerster, H. and Nevison, D. (1992) *Learning Should Pay*, British Petroleum

Buxton, A., Mayes, D. and Murfin, A. (1994) 'Research and development and trading performance', in A. Buxton, P. Chapman and P. Temple (eds) *Britain's Economic Performance*, Routledge

Confederation of British Industry (1989) *Towards a Skills Revolution*, Confederation of British Industry

Coopers and Lybrand Associates (1985) *Challenge to Complacency: Changing Attitudes to Training*, Manpower Services Commission/National Economic Development Office

Employment Department, *Training Statistics*, various issues, HMSO

Finegold, D. and Soskice, D. (1988) 'The failure of training in Britain: analysis and prescription', *Oxford Review of Economic Policy*, vol. 4, no. 3

Freeman, R. (1995) 'The limits of wage flexibility to curing unemployment', *Oxford Review of Economic Policy*, vol. 11, no. 1

Gallie, D. and White, M. (1993) *Employee Commitment and the Skills Revolution*, Policy Studies Institute

Gardiner, J. (1995) 'Alert sounds on volunteer programmes', *Times Educational Supplement*, 12 May

Goold, M. and Campbell, A. (1986) *Strategies and Styles: The Role of the Centre in Managing Diversified Corporations*, Blackwell

Hawkins, J. and Steedman, H. (1993) 'Mathematics in vocational training for the building trades in Britain, France and Germany' (mimeo)

Keep, E. (1994) 'Vocational education and training for the young', in K. Sisson (ed.) *Personnel Management*, second edition, Blackwell

Keep, E. and Mayhew, K. (1994a) 'Training policy for competitiveness: time for fresh perspective' (mimeo)

Keep, E. and Mayhew, K. (1994b) 'Skilling the jobless: time for a new deal?' *Employment Policy Institute Economic Report*, vol. 8, no. 1

Keep, E. and Mayhew, K. (1995) 'UK training policy: assumptions and reality', in A. Booth and D. Snower (eds) *The Skills Gap and Economic Activity*, Cambridge University Press, Cambridge

Marsh, P. (1990) *Short Termism on Trial*, Institutional Fund Managers Association

Millward, N. (1994) *The New Industrial Relations*, Policy Studies Institute, London

Morris, J., Bacon, N., Blyton, P. and Franz, H. W. (1991) 'Beyond survival: the influence of new forms of work organization in the UK and German steel industries' (mimeo)

Nickell, S. J. and Bond, S. (1995) 'The collapse in demand for the unskilled and the unemployed across the OECD', *Oxford Review of Economic Policy*, vol. 11, no. 1

Oulton, N. (1995) 'Workforce skills and export competitiveness', in A. Booth and D. Snower (eds) *The Skills Gap and Economic Activity*, Cambridge University Press, Cambridge

Prais, S. (1989) 'How Europe would see the new British initiative for standardising vocational qualifications' *National Institute Economic Review*, vol. 129, pp. 52–4

Prais, S. (1990) *Productivity, Education and Training*, National Institute for Economic and Social Research, London

Prais, S. (1991) 'Vocational qualifications in Britain and Europe: theory and practice', *National Institute Economic Review*, May

Sisson, K. (1994) 'Personnel management: paradigms, practice and prospects', in K. Sisson (ed.), *Personnel Management*, second edition, Blackwell, Oxford

Smithers, A. (1993) *All Our Futures: Britain's Educational Revolution*, Manchester University, Centre for Education and Employment Research

Soskice, D. W. (1993) 'Social skills from mass higher education: rethinking the company-based initial training paradigm', *Oxford Review of Economic Policy*, vol. 9, no. 3

Stevens, M. (1994) 'A theoretical model of on-the-job training with imperfect competition', *Oxford Economic Papers*, vol. 46, no. 4

Wood, A. (1994) *North-South Trade, Employment and Inequality*, Oxford University Press

The cost of unemployment and reflections on employment programmes

John Philpott

Introduction

Labour market analysts are often asked to estimate the level and cost of unemployment. Both tasks are more difficult than often imagined. The measurement of unemployment, for example, depends crucially on how one defines the problem. Should one count as unemployed all those people without a job who say they want one, or only those who are actively searching for a job? Similarly, when estimating the cost of unemployment, should one focus solely on the most obvious monetary costs or include also any monetary and non-monetary costs that might result from the effects of unemployment on crime and ill health, etc? Questions such as these bedevil attempts to measure the 'true' level of unemployment and count the 'total cost'; the best that can realistically be hoped for is an approximation based on chosen definitions and assumptions.

This chapter is similar in method and scope to several previous studies of the economic and/or wider costs of unemployment (see for example, House of Lords, 1982; Hakim, 1982; Sinfield and Fraser, 1985; Junankar, 1986; Piachaud, 1994). The first part examines the economic costs of unemployment and includes an estimate of the cost to the Exchequer. The second part then looks at the wider costs of unemployment, focusing upon the links with ill health and crime. The final section sets the cost of unemployment alongside the cost of programmes designed to help unemployed people (especially the long-term unemployed) back to work.

The economic costs of unemployment

The economic costs of unemployment can be considered from the viewpoint of the individual unemployed person or society as a whole. The cost imposed on society is the loss of output of goods and services (Gross Domestic Product, GDP) resulting from the under-utilisation of labour. The cost to the unemployed individual is the income he or she loses when not employed. It is important to note that the individual's loss is the share of the output loss that falls upon the individual, i.e. it should not be added to the output loss. In practice this burden is reduced by the transfer of income from employed individuals to the unemployed through the taxation and benefit systems. Transfer payments form part of the Exchequer cost of unemployment. In addition, the Exchequer bears part of the burden of the output loss in the form of reduced tax receipts.

In examining the various dimensions of the economic cost of unemployment, the following analysis ignores throughout what are sometimes called the benefits (i.e. advantages) of unemployment. Clearly, the welfare of society amounts to more than measured GDP. In principle, unemployment could be said to convey a benefit to society, in the form of increased leisure, that should be set against any output loss. At the level of the individual, increased leisure should to some extent compensate for any loss of income from employment. However, treating increased leisure as a gain in this way seems justifiable only insofar as people are voluntarily unemployed – as we shall discuss below, unemployment more commonly increases various forms of personal and social distress. Obviously some proportion of the unemployed will in some sense be voluntarily unemployed. However, in view of the difficulties (conceptually and empirically) of measuring the extent of voluntary unemployment, we ignore the possible benefits of unemployment.

The output cost of unemployment

The output cost of unemployment can be estimated in several ways. The simplest is to assume that every person who is unemployed would, if employed, produce as much as the average person in employment. The output cost is then calculated by multiplying the average product of labour by the number of people unemployed. Matters are complicated, however, by the fact that it is far from certain how much output would be produced by unemployed people if they were to be placed in jobs. It is not always obvious what sorts of jobs unemployed people would perform, but it is unlikely that an unemployed person will be as productive as the average person in work.

Despite the encroachment of unemployment into the domain of skilled, professional and technical workers, the highest incidence of unemployment remains among the less skilled. Moreover, the experience of unemployment – especially long-term unemployment – may itself deplete the productive potential of unemployed people. Rather than base estimates of the output cost of unemployment on a measure of what people in work produce, it is therefore preferable to estimate the value of the output that an unemployed person might produce. This, of course, requires an element of subjective judgement, but a guideline is provided by official survey data – obtained in the late 1980s – which detail the incomes of people in and out of work (Erens and Hedges, 1990). These data cover the inflow to unemployment (i.e. people becoming unemployed) rather than the stock of unemployed people (including the long-term unemployed). They nonetheless provide the best guide we have to the relative earning power of unemployed people. The data suggest that, if employed, the average unemployed person could expect to earn two-thirds of the average full-time wage. If we take the relative earnings of the unemployed as a measure of their potential output compared with that of the average employed person, we can produce an adjusted estimate of the output cost of unemployment.

Table 7.1 includes estimates for the period of the 1990s recession and subsequent recovery. GDP is measured at constant 1990 prices, with the output cost of unemployment shown both in absolute terms and as a percentage of GDP.

The measure of unemployment used in the analysis is taken from the Department of Employment's quarterly Labour Force Survey (LFS), which is preferred to the Department of Employment's count of people without jobs who are claiming unemployment-related benefits. There are well-known reasons for preferring the LFS measure – which is based on an internationally agreed definition of unemployment as laid down by the International Labour Organisation – to the claimant count. However, during the period covered in the table, both measures indicate a similar level of unemployment. This, of course, raises the question whether both measures of unemployment understate the true level (Royal Statistical Society, 1995).

Table 7.1 The output cost of unemployment, 1989–1994

	GDP (1990 prices) £bn	Output per person employed £000	Unemployment (ILO measure)	Adjusted output loss £bn	Output loss as % GDP
1989	476.2	17.97	2.01	23.8	5.0
1990	478.9	17.94	1.90	22.5	4.7
1991	468.9	18.10	2.33	27.8	5.9
1992	466.6	18.37	2.74	33.2	7.1
1993	476.4	19.06	2.91	36.6	7.6
1994	495.1	19.80	2.71	35.5	7.1

Note: Output per person employed is GDP divided by 'employed labour force' (employees, self-employed and HM Forces). Unemployment measure refers to Spring of each year (LFS data were available only on an annual basis until 1992).

Source: Department of Employment, Employment Gazette

The LFS measure, for example, at present excludes almost a million people who state that they want a job but who, for one reason or another, are not actively searching for a job. The extent to which such people should be counted as unemployed is a matter of controversy. Some analysts argue that there is a large amount of 'disguised unemployment' among the people who are economically inactive – many of whom are living on invalidity benefit (Wells, 1994; see also Balls and Gregg, 1993). Rather than make an estimate of disguised unemployment, however, we have decided to rely upon the LFS measure, but recognise that this may bias downwards our estimates of the output cost of unemployment. In this respect it is worth mentioning the well-known observation – first made by Okun (1962) – that any percentage change in unemployment will lead to a larger percentage change in output. One reason for this is that hidden unemployment falls when the labour market is buoyant and vice versa.

Table 7.1 suggests that the output cost of unemployment in 1994 amounted to over £35 billion, 7 per cent of GDP (measured at 1990 prices). It is important to stress that this lost output is never recouped. The total loss of output due to unemployment between 1990 and 1994 amounts to around a third of GDP in 1994. This offers some indication of the sheer waste associated with unemployment. This is not, of course, to say that the recession and the resulting unemployment could necessarily have been avoided, albeit the causes and duration of the recession are linked to errors of macro-economic policy. However, it does put into perspective the notion of unemployment being a 'price well worth paying' in the battle against inflation.

The suggestion that the cost of unemployment ought to be set against the benefits of low (or lower) inflation does, however, raise the question of how much unemployment should be tolerated. Moving from the current (1995) level of just over two million unemployed to zero unemployment would eliminate the output cost, but would undoubtedly generate considerable inflation. All market economies must tolerate some unemployment simply to allow the labour market to function effectively; even during the post-war era of 'full employment' in Britain, the unemployment rate stood at around 2–3 per cent of the workforce. A more precise estimate of the output cost of unemployment thus requires in turn some estimate of how far unemployment exceeds an achievable and sustainable minimum.

The key words here are achievable and minimum. It might be argued from the experience of recent economic cycles that Britain's current sustainable level of unemployment (i.e. that consistent with stable inflation) is close to the current level. On a strict interpretation one might by extension conclude that the associated output loss is the unavoidable cost of low inflation. However, while it may prove difficult to reduce unemployment below this level by way of expansionary macro-economic measures, there appears to be scope for the use of structural/supply side measures to reduce the sustainable level. We shall return below to the question of whether and how far unemployment can be reduced below the current sustainable rate.

Cost of unemployment to the individual

The output cost shows the extent to which society as a whole loses because of unemployment. But the biggest losers are unemployed people themselves. Although part of the burden of unemployment is shifted from jobless people onto the taxpayer by way of the provision of unemployment-related benefits, people who are without jobs incur a substantial loss of income. One way of estimating the cost to the individual is to calculate a 'replacement ratio' which relates an individual's past or prospective earnings to their benefit income when unemployed.

Unfortunately, the calculation of replacement ratios is far from straightforward since so much depends on the individual circumstances of unemployed people. The usual practice is to calculate ratios for certain categories of broad hypothetical groups, which can then be considered illustrative of individual circumstances (see Table 7.2). The table gives the lie to the sometimes heard suggestion that people are 'better off' on the dole. Although some unemployed people on benefit – especially those with several dependent children – undoubtedly fall into the 'unemployment trap' and face a financial disincentive to take a job, unemployment generally imposes a large financial penalty. Moreover, the replacement ratios in Table 7.2 – which relate to 1991–92 – offer only a snapshot or static account of the income situation of unemployed people. Unemployed people may suffer a long-run income loss if a spell of unemployment reduces their prospective earnings and employment opportunities. This will be a particular problem for people who eventually flow into long-term unemployment. The prospect of permanent social exclusion then compounds the severe financial hardship caused by a prolonged period on benefit.

It is also important to note that unemployed people on benefit (whether short-term or long-term unemployed) have over time experienced a relative – and sometimes absolute – deterioration in living standards. The report of the Joseph Rowntree Foundation's Inquiry into Income and Wealth notes how the relative value of benefits for the unemployed has fallen since the late 1970s, a fact noted also by Piachaud (1994) who calculates that the real level of benefits for unemployed people aged under 25 fell by a quarter between 1979 and 1993.

Table 7.2 Comparisons of weekly incomes in and out of work, 1991–92

	Benefit income £	Net earnings in work £	Replacement ratio %	Share of male unemployed %
Single	67.35	139.28	48	53
Married (0 child)	89.55	185.47	48	18
Married (1 child)	120.95	163.72	74	10
Married (2 child)	142.70	173.79	82	11
Married (3 child)	162.45	192.80	84	5
Married (4 child)	180.00	215.14	84	3

Note: Benefit figure includes housing benefit minus 20 per cent community charge; earnings figure is net earnings minus community charge.

Source: Layard and Philpott (1991)

The Rowntree report finds that this change in benefit provision and the much higher levels of unemployment in the 1980s and 1990s are two of the key factors underlying the sharp rise in income inequality in recent years. Piachaud reports a threefold increase over the 1980s in the number of people on below half average income due to unemployment. He highlights, in particular, the relative and often absolute poverty suffered by people in families with an unemployed head.

The cost of unemployment to the Exchequer

When most people talk about the cost of unemployment, what they have in mind is the Exchequer cost (the 'cost to the Government'). This will include a number of expenditure items and a number of lost revenue items. The key expenditure cost is that of providing and administering unemployment-related benefits. On the revenue side the key 'costs' are lost employee taxes, lost employers' national insurance contributions and lost indirect taxes. It is important to recognise that these Exchequer costs represent the taxpayers' share of the output cost of unemployment as discussed earlier – they should not be added to the output cost. The Government does, however, incur some extra resource costs over and above these, including expenditure on special measures designed to help unemployed people into jobs and any spending (such as that on the National Health Service or the criminal justice system) that is incurred as a result of unemployment.

The Government does not publish a figure for the Exchequer cost of unemployment. Official figures are available for expenditure on the benefit system. However, both the Treasury and the Department of Employment refuse to publish estimates of taxes foregone based on hypothetical assumptions about the potential earnings, personal circumstances and expenditure patterns of unemployed people. Likewise, the Government disputes independent estimates of the Exchequer costs of unemployment, such as those made by the House of Lords (1982), Layard and Philpott (1991), the Unemployment Unit (1993) and most recently Piachaud (1994). Table 7.3 provides an estimate of the Exchequer costs of unemployment in 1994. The estimated cost – £22 billion or over £8,000 per person unemployed – amounts to around two-thirds of the Public Sector Borrowing Requirement in 1994–95. The estimate makes no allowance for the possibility (as mentioned earlier) that some people on invalidity benefits, etc. represent a group of disguised unemployed. Piachaud (1994) estimates that £4 billion could be added to the Exchequer cost of unemployment in 1994 because of unemployment-induced spending on benefits for the sick and disabled.

The wider costs of unemployment

Many studies have examined possible links between unemployment, personal distress, ill health, and wider social problems such as increased crime. This chapter offers a brief review of the available evidence. More detailed reviews of the association between unemployment and ill health are provided by Smith (1987), Taylor (1991), Fryer (1992) and the Office of Health Economics (1993). Piachaud (1994) and Wells (1995) review the major evidence of a link between unemployment and crime.

Unemployment and health

There is a clear statistical association between unemployment and a variety of measures of ill health. The key task for researchers has been to establish whether there is a causal link running from unemployment to ill health – as opposed to ill health making people more prone to unemployment. The other question is the degree to which health problems emerge because of the poverty that is often associated with unemployment, rather than simply unemployment itself.

Table 7.3 Exchequer cost of unemployment, UK 1994[1]

	£ million
Benefits[2]	10,003
Administration of benefits[3]	737
Statutory redundancy payments and administration[4]	222
Direct taxes	4,581
Employers' national insurance contributions	3,371
Indirect taxes	3,164
Total	22,078

(Total per person unemployed: £8,429)

Notes

1. The figures for lost tax revenues are taken from Piachaud (1994). It is assumed that the unemployed would, if employed, earn two-thirds of average earnings. Direct tax losses were estimated by applying the average tax rate for the bottom quintile of non-retired households to the lost earnings. Tax foregone on unemployment benefits (assuming all unemployment benefit is taxed at the basic rate) was deducted. Lost employers' NI contributions were estimated at 10 per cent of earnings. Loss of indirect taxes was estimated by applying the average burden of indirect tax to the loss of disposable income suffered by unemployed people.

2. Figures derived from the Total Benefit Expenditure on Unemployed People in Cash Terms in *Department of Social Security Statistics*, HMSO.

3. Taken from *The Government's Expenditure Plans 1995–96 to 1997–98*, Employment Department Group, HMSO.

4. Taken from *The Government's Expenditure Plans 1995–96 to 1997–98*, Employment Department Group, HMSO.

The clearest links are with mental health. Studies by economists and psychologists agree that unemployment causes increased mental distress (unemployed people are unhappy, Clark and Oswald, 1994; Jahoda, 1979; Warr, 1987). Although work itself can sometimes cause stress, it provides income, routine, status and social contacts. The loss of work results in low self-esteem, depression and damaged social and family life. It is found, for example, that the chances that a person's marriage will dissolve increases by over two-thirds in the year following a bout of unemployment (Lampard, 1994; Hakim, 1982). Having said this, considerable variation is found in the degree to which people are affected by unemployment. Indeed, some people even experience an improvement in mental health (Fryer, 1992). The effect on individuals seems to depend upon the amount of financial strain imposed, the extent to which they were committed to their previous employment, and whether they have what might be called a 'hinterland' of non-work interests and associations. There is no apparent difference between blue-collar and white-collar workers in the amount of distress experienced, although gender differences are observed. Married women – who bear the bulk of domestic responsibilities – suffer less than men. The same is not true of unemployed single women, who experience similar levels of stress to their male counterparts (Warr and Parry, 1982). Besides these direct effects, high unemployment is found to increase stress levels among people in work, especially those at risk of redundancy (Gore, 1978).

Clark and Oswald (1994) find that distress levels are lower for younger than older workers, lower in areas of high unemployment, and lower among the long-term unemployed. The latter finding is perhaps surprising, but broadly consistent with psychological studies. In all cases, however, unemployed people are more distressed than people with jobs. Whether this leads to higher rates of suicide and parasuicide (i.e. deliberate self-harm), however, is a matter of some controversy. There is a well-documented statistical association between unemployment and suicide attempts (Platt and Kreitman, 1984), but epidemiologists have been generally reluctant to commit themselves to attribute causation because many unemployed people who attempt suicide have been found to have a previous history of psychiatric treatment.

Also controversial are the supposed links between unemployment and physical ill health, partly because of the difficulty of separating effects on illness due to unemployment from those that result from poverty and disadvantage more generally. A link has, however, been established between unemployment and increased morbidity. A study of men unemployed in the week before the 1971 census found that unemployment raised the chances that a man would die in the following ten years by around a third (Moser *et al*, 1984). Whatever the precise link between unemployment and health, there is an association between unemployment and the consumption of health-care resources. The Office of Health Economics (1993) notes (from the General Household Survey) that GP consultation rates are 20 per cent higher for unemployed people. Based on this finding, the OHE estimates that in 1992 unemployment cost the NHS £40 million in higher GP and pharmaceutical services, plus £30.6 million in lost revenue since unemployed people are entitled to free medical prescriptions. The total estimated cost of £71 million (or roughly £24 per unemployed person at that time) excluded any hospital services for the unemployed.

Unemployment and crime

Crime is costly. The victims suffer materially, psychologically and possibly physically. There is an opportunity cost to consumers who have to take crime-prevention measures (e.g. buy burglar alarms), and resources have to be devoted to maintaining the criminal justice system. But to what extent can the costs of crime be said to be caused by unemployment? It is certainly true that crime generally has been on an upward trend in Britain since the era of mass unemployment began in the mid-1970s, and it is well known that property crime rises and falls in line with changes in economic activity. Yet clearly not all unemployed people resort to crime, and not all criminals are unemployed. So what is the evidence of a link running from unemployment to crime?

Home Office research finds no causal relation between unemployment and property crime over the economic cycle once changes in consumption behaviour are accounted for, although there does appear to be some association between long-term unemployment and crimes of violence against the person (Field, 1990). The finding for property crime has been challenged on methodological grounds by Wells (1995). It can be argued that the Home Office study does not take account of the fact that unemployment is a lagging indicator of conditions in the economy, nor does it adjust adequately for inadequacies in the claimant count as a measure of unemployment. Moreover, many studies in both the US and Britain indicate a strong link between unemployment, social disadvantage and crime (Chiricos, 1987; Freeman, 1993; Dickinson 1994).

Case studies suggest that groups most prone to unemployment may also be those more likely to turn to crime (Farrington *et al*, 1986). Similarly, the tendency for unemployed young men to commit burglary seems to be exacerbated by low educational attainment and poor economic opportunities (Dickinson, 1994). It would seem likely, therefore, that the temptation to resort to crime is greatest in those pockets of society where access to resources is limited and the short-run prospect of income from legitimate employment is bleak. In such a situation, as Dickinson contends, unemployment may be sufficient to erode the social constraints on crime.

The Crime and Social Policy Committee (1995) makes a similar point, linking crime with changes in the labour market more generally. The choice facing young men with little education and few skills is often long-term unemploy-ment or low-wage/low-quality employment. The Committee argues that the financial incentive to commit crime may be increasing for such individuals, while the 'opportunity cost' of being caught, in terms of lost earnings, is falling. One implication of this is that solutions to unemployment that rely largely on the creation of more low-wage jobs for the unskilled may do little to reduce crime (see also Freeman, 1993 and Freeman, 1995).

A related factor in the relationship between crime, unemployment and conditions in the labour market may be drug use. Piachaud (1994) cites a study from one area of North-West England that indicates that drug use is higher where unemployment is higher and notes that drug users may resort to crime to finance the habit. In the US, drug-related crime is driven up by disadvantaged youths turning to the often lucrative practice of drug dealing as an alternative to the legitimate labour market (Freeman, 1993).

Whatever the precise link between unemployment and crime, it would appear that higher unemployment has raised the criminal justice bill simply because unemployed offenders are more likely to be imprisoned than fined. In the 1970s, when unemployment was lower, fines typically accounted for 50 per cent of sentences for indictable offences. By the end of the 1980s this proportion had fallen to around 40 per cent (Lea-Wilson, 1992). Coles and Fowles (1991) combine evidence that the size of the prison population is related to unemployment with a calculation of the weekly cost of imprisonment, to estimate that a 1 per cent increase in the unemployment rate costs the Home Office £1 million.

Reflections on employment programmes

The cost of unemployment must be seen in the light of feasible solutions. For example, if nothing could be done to reduce the rate of structural unemployment, society would have to tolerate the associated loss of output. The choice facing society would then become one of whether and how to redistribute available work and income, i.e. how to spread the burden of unemployment more evenly between social groups and individuals. Issues of distribution should, of course, be at the forefront of economic and social policy debate whatever the level of unemployment. But it seems unduly pessimistic to accept the current rate of structural unemployment as a *fait accompli*. So what might be done to get more people into jobs, creating extra output?

Unemployment is a complex problem with more than one cause and with no single or simple solution. Many economists, however, argue that the structural unemployment problem in Britain and Europe has been exacerbated by the way in which unemployment benefit systems operate (Layard *et al*, 1991; Snower, 1994 and 1995; for a review of the evidence and arguments see OECD, 1994 and Blondal and Pearson, 1995). In particular it is argued that inefficient unemployment benefit systems foster long-term unemployment, thereby creating a large group of 'outsiders' in the labour market who find it difficult to obtain jobs even when demand is buoyant and, crucially, bear no disciplining influence on the wage demands of employed 'insiders'. Consequently long-term unemployment – which currently accounts for almost 40 per cent of total unemployment in Britain – serves no anti-inflationary role. Thus, the output loss associated with long-term unemployment can be considered a complete waste in economic terms.

The conclusion normally drawn from this is that a combination of welfare reform and the use of more active labour market measures targeted at the long-term unemployed could help cut unemployment substantially without causing an upsurge in inflation. At the same time it would generate additional output of economic, social and community value . Moreover, there is a strong argument that whatever the precise impact of active measures on the level of unemployment, extra help for the jobless is justified on equity grounds, since this is targeted at the most disadvantaged groups and individuals in the labour market. A broad consensus has thus developed in official and unofficial policy circles that more of the resources devoted to maintaining unemployed people on benefit (so-called 'passive measures') should be redirected towards active measures such as job search, training, and job subsidy or public job-creation programmes (European Commission, 1993; OECD, 1994; Commission on Social Justice, 1994; Joseph Rowntree Foundation, 1995; ILO, 1995). However, there are marked differences of opinion about the precise use and effectiveness of such measures and, above all, about the efficacy of expanding job subsidies or job-creation measures on a very large scale.

Active labour market policies

The UK Government is currently spending annually some £2 billion of taxpayers' money on employment and training programmes directed at unemployed adults (Employment Department, 1995). The history of such programmes goes back many years and priorities have changed over time (Philpott, 1991). The present emphasis is on a plethora of job-search programmes operated by the Employment Service. More expensive adult-training programmes – organised by the Training and Enterprise Councils – by contrast face budgetary cutback in the next few years. Temporary community jobs programmes – the vogue in the mid-1980s but later superseded by an emphasis on training – are back in fashion, albeit on a far more modest scale than in the past. The same is true of job subsidies, although their present use has been restricted to Workstart pilot schemes, designed to test ways of combating 'discrimination' against the long-term unemployed in the recruitment process.

n addition, the 1994 Budget announced a number of 'welfare to work' measures, including a one-year national insurance holiday – to be introduced in 996 – for employers who hire the two-year-plus unemployed (Philpott, 1994).

t is often argued that job subsidies, 'benefit transfers', or temporary community obs programmes designed to support long-term unemployed people in mployment could be expanded considerably and at no additional cost to the xchequer – certainly in the medium term – once savings in benefit payments nd tax revenue 'flowbacks' are accounted for (Layard and Philpott, 1991; nower, 1994). This looks like a 'free lunch'. The Government, however, refuses o sit down to eat. Indeed, the Secretary of State for Employment recently went o far as to label proponents of such arguments 'three-card tricksters' (Portillo, 995).

he Government points to the fact that employment programmes suffer from he well-known problem of deadweight, and produce job substitution and lisplacement effects. Taking such problems into account, the net effect of an mployment programme on unemployment will generally be less than the umber of people supported by the programme. This raises the cost per dditional job created. It is quite possible for the cost per additional job to xceed any savings in benefit and tax flowbacks, resulting in a net cost to the xchequer. If employment programmes do have a net cost, they must be inanced by cuts in other forms of public spending, or by higher taxation or orrowing. This will have implications for jobs elsewhere in the economy, and ossibly also longer-run consequences for the overall performance of the conomy (Employment Department, 1993).

fficial evaluations of job subsidies in the 1980s suggest a net cost per person emoved from unemployment of between £3,500 and £4,000 (at 1993–94 prices). his is slightly higher than the cost of each place on the Community Programme emporary jobs scheme (£3,300), which operated until 1988 (Philpott, 1993). The verall implication of financing such programmes thus depends to a large extent n their scale (which may in turn also determine the extent to which the output nd employment generated by programmes displace other output and mployment). Advocates of larger-scale use of active labour market policies, owever, counter such estimates of the likely cost. For one thing, the cost of rogrammes can be reduced by better targeting and programme design. But, n addition, it can be argued that official evaluations of programmes are too artial in scope and in particular take too narrow a view of substitution and lisplacement effects (Layard *et al*, 1991).

If providing jobs for the long-term unemployed does not affect the amount of unemployment needed to keep wage inflation in check, any associated rise in the pool of short-term unemployed caused by job substitution or displacement will exert downward pressure on wage growth. This will in turn lead to more jobs being created. The length of the adjustment period may be uncertain, although ideally it would be speeded up by the Government relaxing macro-economic policy in line with the reduction in wage pressure. However, the ultimate effect of helping the long-term unemployed is to expand the effective supply of labour and to cut total unemployment without raising short-term unemployment. Therefore, so long as the gross cost of programmes does not exceed the cost of unemployment to the Exchequer, programmes should be self-financing and may even save money.

Interestingly, in defending the pilot Workstart subsidy, the former Secretary of State for Employment acknowledged that the aim of the subsidy is to expand the supply of labour in exactly the way that advocates of large-scale active labour market policies suggest. Yet Mr Portillo continued to deny that it is possible for the State to create extra jobs for the long-term unemployed at no additional cost (Portillo, 1995). It seems difficult to envisage a reconciliation of views on this issue without a large-scale experiment. Any such 'experiment' would presumably have to involve a significant sub-group of the long-term unemployed, such as all those aged 18–24.

It could, of course, be argued that the State should try to create or subsidise more jobs even if this did involve some net cost, on the grounds that this would be 'a price worth paying' to cut unemployment (Glyn, 1995). Such an argument takes us beyond economics *per se* and into the realms of political economy. A very crude estimate – based on conventional analysis – would suggest that a wholesale attempt to tackle long-term unemployment by creating temporary jobs in the public/voluntary sectors or subsidising private sector jobs might require extra (i.e. net) public spending of around £4 billion per annum. This is not a major sum in total public finance terms, but neither is it trivial. If financed by borrowing, for example, £4 billion would have added over 10 per cent to the 1994–95 Public Sector Borrowing Requirement. Assuming, however, that the Government would not be prepared to fund such spending by higher borrowing or cutting other public programmes, the burden would have to fall on the taxpayer (adding, say, the equivalent of 2 pence in the pound to the standard rate of income tax).

In effect, therefore, a policy of job creation designed to cut long-term unem-ployment that incurred a net cost would entail a redistribution of income from 'insiders' to formerly unemployed 'outsiders' (with the consumption of the latter when placed in jobs compensating for any reduced consumption by the former when more highly taxed). The success of the policy would depend crucially upon the willingness of taxpayers to bear the cost. In this regard, emphasis on the benefits of lower unemployment – for example higher output of public or private services and reduced social problems – offers one possible 'sales pitch' for policy makers. The sales task would be aided by constructing a 'social rate of return' for employment programmes. Alternatively, policy makers could place most stress on the moral or social justice case for cutting unemployment (Dilnot and Blastland, 1995). The latter argument becomes stronger if it is assumed that the value of potential output of most unemployed people – and especially the long-term unemployed – is fairly low and that the main benefit to flow from lower unemployment is greater social cohesion. But either way, any policy to cut unemployment that required a distribution from the 'haves' to the 'have nots' would have to be based on some measure of social consensus. In the absence of this, taxpayers will either resist tax increases through the ballot box or (as employed 'insiders') press for compensatory wage rises which could sabotage the entire job-creation exercise.

Some final thoughts on programme design

When discussing the issue of employment programmes for the long-term unemployed, the report of the Joseph Rowntree Foundation's Inquiry into Income and Wealth suggests that programmes will only be worthwhile if the jobs created have a clear purpose, involve training and offer a clear financial advantage for participants, and if participation is voluntary. Such suggestions for programme design raise important questions. As a caveat to the preceding discussion, for example, it is worth noting the observation that the expansion of active labour market policies in Sweden in the 1980s may have raised wage pressure (Calmfors, 1993). This may have been because Swedish jobs programmes at the time operated on the principle of offering a market 'rate for the job', which made them attractive in comparison with regular employment. To minimise the danger that employment programmes might reduce rather than increase work incentives and active job search, Calmfors thus argues that rates of pay should be substantially lower than market rates. This view is shared by the OECD (1994), which recommends that payments to participants should be as close as possible to benefit levels and that participation could be made part-time to release time for job search. This is a controversial recommendation – though quite close to current UK practice – as is the OECD's corresponding recommendation that long-term benefits should be made conditional on participation in active labour market programmes.

Turning to training, it may be a mistake to seek to introduce a training element to all employment programmes for the long-term unemployed. The objectives of training programmes extend beyond those of job subsidies or job-creation programmes. The principal objectives are to raise the long-run employment and earnings potential of participants, and reduce any shorter-run skills shortages that might be adding to wage pressure in the labour market.

Available international evidence on the effectiveness of training is equivocal. Calmfors and Skedinger (1995), for example, draw the tentative conclusion that training programmes in Sweden had more favourable macro-economic effects than job-creation programmes, but note that this may have been because training allowances were lower than rates of pay on employment programmes.

More generally, available evidence indicates that broadly targeted training programmes are less effective than training measures directed specifically at groups for which it is possible to attribute identifiable training needs (OECD, 1994) The worst approach may be where training is offered as an entitlement to large numbers of unemployed people as an alternative to benefit. It may well be that in this narrow programmatic sense 'training' has been grossly oversold as a solution to unemployment. Despite the criticism of cuts in the public training budget in the UK, it may be that a relatively small but increasingly more focused programme, such as Training for Work (which will provide 120,000 training places this year) offers the best available approach (Robinson, 1994 and 1995). However, the record of this programme for job placement and provision of recognised qualifications – though improving – remains poor. A fundamental independent review of how best to deliver training to the long-term unemployed is long overdue. Far more effort and energy appear devoted to drawing up often broad-brush proposals for tackling long-term unemployment than to the more mundane but ultimately crucial questions of programme design and management. In this respect the following conclusion of the OECD (1994) seems fully justified:

> The types of measures needed and their design and day to day management constantly raise new challenges which, if not addressed, can easily lead to routine programmes where unemployed people are simply 'held' for a while without their job prospects being improved. In sum, the clear advantage of active labour market policies over 'passive' income support will only come into play if there is a strong political commitment to these programmes and effective management of them.

References

Balls, E. and Gregg, P. (1993) *Work and Welfare*, Commission on Social Justice/ Institute for Public Policy Research

Blondal, S. and Pearson, M. (1995) 'Unemployment and other non-employment benefits', *Oxford Review of Economic Policy*, vol. 11, no. 1, Spring

Calmfors, L. (1993) 'Lessons from the macroeconomic experience of Sweden', *European Journal of Political Economy*, vol. 9, no. 1, March

Calmfors, L. and Skedinger, P. (1995) 'Does active labour market policy increase employment? Theoretical considerations and some empirical evidence from Sweden', *Oxford Review of Economic Policy*, vol. 11, no. 1, Spring

Chiricos, T. (1987) 'Rates of crime and unemployment', *Social Problems*, vol. 34, no. 2

Clark, A. and Oswald, A. (1994) 'Unhappiness and unemployment', *Economic Journal*, vol. 104, May

Coles, A. and Fowles, A. (1991) *Unemployment, Crime, Offenders and their Training*, Department of Social Policy, University of York

Commission on Social Justice (1994) *Social Justice: Strategies for National Renewal*, IPPR/Vintage

Crime and Social Policy Committee (1995) *Crime and Social Policy*, NACRO

Dickinson, D. (1994) *Crime and Unemployment* (mimeo), University of Cambridge Department of Applied Economics

Dilnot, A. and Blastland, M. (1995) 'The moral case for cutting joblessness', *Financial Times*, 22 June

Employment Department (1993) *Memorandum to the House of Commons Employment Select Committee Inquiry into the Employment Consequences of British Coal's Proposed Pit Closure Programme*, HMSO

Employment Department (1995) *The Government's Expenditure Plans 1995–96 to 1997–98, Employment Department Group Report*, HMSO, March

Erens, B. and Hedges, B. (1990) *Survey of Incomes In and Out of Work*, HMSO

European Commission (1993) *Growth, Competitiveness and Employment*, Brussels

Farrington D. and others (1986) 'Unemployment, school leaving and crime', *British Journal of Criminology*, vol. 26

Field, S. (1990) *Trends in Crime and Their Interpretation: A Study of Recorded Crime in England and Wales*, Home Office Research Study 119

Freeman, R. (1993) *Crime and the Unemployment of Disadvantaged Youths*, Centre for Economic Performance Working Paper

Freeman, R. (1995) 'The limits of wage flexibility to curing unemployment', *Oxford Review of Economic Policy*, vol. 11, no. 1, Spring

Fryer, D. (1992) 'Psychological or material deprivation: why does unemployment have mental health consequences?' in E. McLauglin (ed.) *Understanding Unemployment*, Routledge

Glyn, A. (1995) 'The assessment: unemployment and inequality', *Oxford Review of Economic Policy*, vol. 11, no. 1, Spring

Gore, D. (1978) 'The effect of social support in moderating the health consequences of unemployment', *Health and Social Behaviour*

Hakim, C. (1982) 'The social consequences of high unemployment', *Journal of Social Policy*, vol. 11, no. 4

House of Lords (1982) *Report from the Select Committee on Unemployment*, HMSO

International Labour Organisation (1995) *World Employment Report*, Geneva

Jahoda, M. (1979) 'The impact of unemployment in the 1930s and 1980s', *Bulletin of British Psychological Society*, vol. 32

Joseph Rowntree Foundation (1995) *Joseph Rowntree Foundation Inquiry into Income and Wealth*, vols 1 and 2, JRF, York

Junankar, P. N. (1986) *Cost of Unemployment*, European Commission

Lampard, R. (1994) 'An examination of the relationship between marital dissolution and unemployment', in D. Gallie (ed.) *Social Change and the Experience of Unemployment*, Oxford University Press

Layard, R., Nickell, S. and Jackman, R. (1991) *Unemployment*, Oxford University Press

Layard, R. and Philpott, J. (1991) *Stopping Unemployment*, Employment Policy Institute

Lea-Wilson, F. (1992) *Sentenced to Unemployment*, Employment Policy Institute Economic Report, vol. 6, no. 9, February

Moser, K., Goldblatt, P.O., Fox, A.J. and Jones, D.R. (1984) 'Unemployment and morbidity in the OPCS longitudinal study', *The Lancet*

OECD (1994) *Jobs Study: Facts, Analysis and Strategies* and *Evidence and Explanations*, Parts I and II

Office of Health Economics (1993) *The Impact of Unemployment on Health*, OHE Briefing no. 29, July

Okun, A. (1962) *Potential GNP: Its Measurement and Significance*, American Statistical Association

Philpott, J. (1992) 'British policies and their effects', in R. Disney and A. Carruth (eds) *Helping the Unemployed*, Anglo-German Foundation

Philpott, J. (1993) *Making Workstart Work*, Employment Policy Institute Economic Report, vol. 7, no. 8, April

Philpott, J. (1994) *Two Cheers for the Chancellor*, Employment Policy Institute Economic Report, vol. 8, no. 10, December

Piachaud, D. (1994) *A Price Worth Paying? The Costs of Mass Unemployment*, Employment Policy Institute Economic Report, vol. 8, no. 6, September

Platt, S. and Kreitman, N. (1984) 'Trends in parasuicide and unemployment among men in Edinburgh, 1964–82', *British Medical Journal*

Portillo, M. (1995) 'You cannot spend your way out of unemployment', Speech by the Secretary of State for Employment to the London Rotary Club, 20 February

Robinson, P. (1994) *The Decline in the Swedish Model and the Limits to Active Labour Market Policies,* Centre for Economic Performance Working Paper 667

Robinson, P. (1995) *The Limits of Active Labour Market Policies,* Employment Policy Institute, vol. 9, no. 6, July

Royal Statistical Society (1995) *Report of the Working Party on the Measurement of Unemployment in the UK*

Sinfield, A. and Fraser, N. (1985) *The Real Cost of Unemployment,* BBC/University of Edinburgh

Smith, R. (1987) *Unemployment and Health,* Oxford University Press

Snower, D. (1994) *Converting Unemployment Benefits into Employment Subsidies,* CEPR Discussion Paper no. 930

Snower, D. (1995) 'Evaluating unemployment policies: what do the underlying theories tell us?' *Oxford Review of Economic Policy*, vol. 11, no. 1, Spring

Taylor, P. (1991) *Unemployment and Health,* Campaign for Work Research Report, vol. 3, no. 6

Unemployment Unit (1993) *Working Brief,* issue 49, November/December

Warr, P. and Parry, G. (1982) 'Paid employment and workers psychological experience', *Psychological Bulletin*, 191

Warr, P. (1987) *Work, Unemployment and Mental Health,* Clarendon Press, Oxford

Wells, J. (1994) *Unemployment in the UK: The Missing Million,* European Labour Forum, no. 13

Wells, J. (1995) *Crime and Unemployment,* Employment Policy Institute Economic Report, vol. 9, no. 1, February

8 Dreaming of work

Ed Mayo

*About six months ago I lost my job. Like millions before me, I found it extremely
difficult to be unemployed. It was a real loss, not unlike a family death, that
affected every corner of my life and relationships. Without a job, I lost something
that applied my skills, I have no role, no trade. I also lost a salary, I am now a
dependant. Finally, because I lost all these things along with my job, I stopped
believing in myself. I could not value the contribution I was making, so I could
not value myself.* (Tony Quibell, Walsall)[1]

Introduction

Mass unemployment and its associated exclusion and poverty is wasteful in
economic terms and a denial of basic human freedoms. But should we assume
that in the 21st century employment will be the answer to unemployment?

Work is something of use or value to the person who does it, or for whom it is
done. Many of the most important and fulfilling parts of our lives – such as
caring, favours and parenting – fit within this description, but are not
predominantly organised as employment.

Employment itself is a modern phenomenon. Just as common land was claimed
by landowners in the enclosure of last century, so work has become enclosed as
employment. Modern development brings into markets work that used to be
non-marketed and assigns a low status to work with no monetary return.

This enclosure of work as employment has meant that the labour market
exclusively defines how we organise *and* validate work within society (where
those out of employment are dismissed as 'economically inactive'). The results?
We have two – twin evils – mass unemployment on the one hand, and a large
amount of socially useful work remaining undone on the other. It is hard to
imagine a worse outcome.

This chapter addresses these two issues in turn. In the case of unemployment, it
is now more widely accepted that there are not, nor likely to be, enough jobs for
all who want them. And further, those on offer are becoming less secure. The
central issue is therefore how people, particularly in deprived neighbourhoods,

can organise their own work to a greater degree. In the case of the second theme the traditional model of economic wealth creation seeks to maximise national income and its distribution through wage labour. A more relevant model for the 21st century is the economy that seeks to optimise human quality of life on an environmentally sustainable basis. The way that we organise, reward and validate work within society therefore needs to maximise its social and environmental, and not simply its monetary, return.

From examples of current and emerging practice that relate to these two issues, I then ask what policies would support these and what the future of work could therefore look like for the 21st century.

The critique of full employment

The progressive, green critique of employment has often seemed either a sideline, an irritation or a dangerous diversion to the concerned and 'vested' interests of the full-employment campaign. This critique, based on the works of writers such as Karl Polanyi and Jeremy Rifkin, charts the historical shift from self-reliance and the 'commons' in pre-industrial times. Such conditions were not romantic. Scarcity was real (and often enough fatal), but was conceived as irregular (Zadek, 1993). In modern times, embodied in the classical economic paradigm, scarcity is recast as absolute and markets become the dominant form of resource allocation. In the field of work, the mode of employment replaces the mode of livelihood, and power relations are increasingly characterised by dependency, as workers are dependent on employers to provide them with jobs. 'Full employment' is viewed as a modern construct, and one of uncertain value in a context of ecological stress, technology trends and trade liberalisation.

André Gorz, in his *Farewell to the Working Class*, takes this story to its fictional end in a scenario where the young unemployed 'for the previous two years had been occupying abandoned plants to engage in "wildcat production" of various socially useful products' (Gorz, 1982).

The prediction of the 'end' of an era of full employment has proved convincing and is now a commonplace view. Rapid change within the labour market has overturned traditional ideas and expectations of what constitutes a 'job', with rising part-time and self-employment and increasing women's participation in the labour market.

Similarly, the concept of livelihood and stress on fostering more self-organised patterns of work fits well with the recent concepts of 'portfolio' work of Charles

Handy and 'you & co.' of William Bridges, and with the 'farmer first' strategy for participative development of Robert Chambers (Handy, 1989; Bridges, 1995; Chambers, 1995). The one is usually seen as relating to the richest people in society, the other the poorest.

Yet the employment lobby has long resisted the critique. Many of today's campaigns for social change (from equal opportunities to collective bargaining) are premised on the institution of the traditional 'job', so that denial is seductive compared to the long hard task of recreating movements and institutions for social change in a new context.

But, for the poorest communities of Europe, the job has already disappeared and given way to a variety of creative coping strategies. It is not enough to sit back and wait for a tide of economic growth to lift the poorest communities back into the labour market. It is not going to happen for the foreseeable future.

Utopias of work and employment

The progressive, green critique has therefore proved resilient, but only up to a point. It may be that, as André Gide wrote, to reach new lands you have to lose sight of the old shore for some time. But the upheaval and insecurity associated with labour market changes over recent years caution against any simplistic assertion that these prefigure an easy shift towards a more positive utopia of work.

Full employment itself should be seen as one such utopia. In its modern variety, the utopia of full employment has its heart in an emphasis on social justice and a right of choice to meaningful employment for men and women. In its traditional form, the utopia of full employment also internalised the 'means' to its end, stressing in particular the role of the State in setting a conducive macro-economic framework.

Such means are clearly unconvincing. The main thrust of the economy will simply not deliver full employment in its current form, and the changes required for it to deliver are global in nature and therefore cannot be expected to happen in the near or far future.

The conversation about growth and employment is over in its traditional form. Economic growth will not rise sufficiently above productivity trends to create enough jobs. Unless output grows at a higher rate than labour productivity, assuming that the labour force remains constant, the UK will still go into the

---

Utopias

Most studies within the employment debate use *data* that contradict or confirm *theories* (empirical thinking). Or they consist of a critical reading of certain *data* as a function of specific *values* (critical thinking). Both methods are good for day-to-day policy making, but a third approach is possible, which out of the present situation looks for creative scenarios or proposals based on *theories* that meet the needs of certain *values* (utopian thinking).

Utopias set direction and play an important role in the history of emancipatory politics, providing space for the 'education of desire'. Without utopias, we couldn't dream. And without dreams, we can't organise for a fairer society.

In future studies, more often than not all three are in play. So, behind extrapolation based on empirical or critical research may be a set of utopian assumptions (including assumptions that nothing else is going to change). Full employment and a socially just society are such utopias, as perhaps is the current mantra of sustainable non-inflationary growth.

---

next recession with 2.5 to 3 million unemployed. Nor, at a European level, will it create enough jobs to cater for a predicted 15 per cent rise in the workforce by 2010 (Griffiths, 1995).

The twin engines of economic globalisation – the development of global capital markets and the liberalisation of trade – remove much of the scope that previously existed for significant national action to promote employment. Transnational companies rarely see themselves as accountable for the social impact of industrial restructuring. The international economy lacks the institutional architecture to enforce such social accountability; nor does it allow any successful co-ordinated programme of monetary reflation.

The conventional employment strategies of left and right will not, on this view, lead to a return to full employment. There is a need not just for action but for innovation.

Reconceiving work

But whatever employment levels pertain in the medium-term, there are good reasons to recast the utopia from one of full employment to one (sometimes dubbed 'full engagement') which provides access to income and to meaningful work, paid or unpaid, for all citizens.

First, for the immediate future, the lead export sectors for the UK – such as financial services, tourism and manufacturing – will remain central to national employment levels and generating secondary employment and income. However, the evidence of 'jobless' communities is on the rise. Trickle-down development is inadequate. But equally, conventional community regeneration, premised on reinserting neighbourhoods back into the mainstream economy, also has a mixed record. So, in the face of mass unemployment there is a pressing need for alternative approaches to work within deprived neighbourhoods that meet people's needs and promote local self-reliance.

At the same time, there is a pressing social and economic need to reverse the low status and conditions of unpaid work, given the increasing stress and personal cost to those doing it. Unpaid work is an essential base on which the rest of our lives rest. It is also a considerable subsidy of effort and time by the poorer sections of society of benefit to the richer. Six million people, for example, identify themselves as carers in the UK (Glendinning and McLaughlin, 1993). This is an issue increasingly making its way up the political agenda, in terms of volunteer schemes, family policy, support for carers and the role of parents in education.

Second, employment should be seen not as an end in itself, but as a means to achieving a better quality of life. This means distinguishing between forms of work, with the aim of promoting patterns of work that are socially useful and contribute to greater personal autonomy and fulfilment (Csikszentmihalyi, 1992; Lane, 1993).

Work in jobless communities

The new localism

Economic globalisation is often described in the image of nature (the centrifugal forces of wind and hurricane) or of battle (competitions and trade wars). Both images exaggerate the real extent of globalisation to date, but also suggest a powerlessness to act at any other level than the global. Yet globalisation is not the end of local action. Rather it creates a new logic for it. Indeed, the most energetic and forward-looking work within both social and environmental movements in Europe and abroad stresses participative research and planning, neighbourhood involvement, decentralisation of services and bootstrap community economic initiatives.

Is it possible to organise work at a local level? One example of how to do this is the growth of Local Exchange Trading Schemes (LETS) since their introduction to the UK through the New Economics Foundation in 1985.

LETS operate by a group of people in a locality, or with a shared interest, forming a local currency and using it to trade in goods and services. The group forms the currency by giving it a name (acorns, bobbins, anchors, etc.) and an initial value. The members then list the goods and services they are offering and wanting, and price them in the local currency. Information about the list can be distributed by a printed directory, notices in a community centre, or even signs outside people's homes. To trade, members then contact each other directly and specify the job. The price is then agreed between them, and payment is made using a LETS cheque.

The transactions are recorded on a PC or ledger by a member who acts as a 'banker', and periodically issues statements showing members' balances. Members do not need to earn LETS before spending them. If their balance shows a minus figure because they have spent more than they have earned, it means that they have committed themselves to doing some more work on LETS in the future. No interest is paid or charged on balances, and the system is regulated by all balances being open to inspection by members.

In economic terms, LETS fulfil the three conventional criteria for money. They are a unit of account, a means of exchange and a store of value (although not a store of capital appreciation). In creating a local currency, they dissolve the traditional (sterling-defined) barrier between the formal and informal economy, and, hence, the traditional distinction between employment and unpaid work. LETS generate a local enhanced multiplier effect, allowing people access to goods and services they might not otherwise have afforded.

The rapid growth of LETS (achieved with virtually no national development grant funding) can be explained by their comparative ease of start-up, a high media profile and strong, open decentralised networks for information sharing. However, LETS are not a solution in themselves. They are part of a new social technology needed to build more sustainable and socially-inclusive communities. LETS now need to develop in ways that allow them to become a livelihood rather than a hobby. This means spreading LETS in low-income communities,[2] adapting them to the needs and opportunities of an ageing population, engaging micro- and small-scale businesses, and convincing the public sector to take a more flexible and creative approach in the treatment of benefits. There is evidence of increasing confidence and capacity among the pioneers within the LETS movement, which augurs well for the slow, detailed negotiations that lie ahead.

Work and telematics

There has been considerable debate about the impact of telematics on work, society and the environment. In general it appears as if initial assumptions, of job losses or environmental gain, soon give way to more measured, if uncertain, conclusions. The 'sunrise' computer industries of California, for example, have been associated with the highest concentration of hazardous clean-up sites in the USA (Robertson, 1995).

In the field of the social economy, telematics has, at least, been used to create or support new models of work and exchange, of which LETS is one example. Electronic trading networks, for example, combine the collaborative advantages of electronic trading schemes with the competitive advantages of network-based markets. Such networks are used, for example, by the Manchester Asian Trading Information Network (MATIN), which was established to build on the ethnic identity of a significant minority in Manchester to promote trade within that and with other parts of the Manchester community (Zadek and Mansell, 1995).

Intermediate labour markets

LETS can be regarded as an intermediate labour market or they can be regarded as an alternative labour market, according to the priorities of those participating. Any argument that they may create a second-class economy that further disconnects low-income communities from the rest of society is at best unproved – and tends to be contradicted by informal evidence of the opposite. LETS should not create the impression of a dualistic structure of classical work versus local exchange. Instead they point towards the multiple ways of organising and rewarding work.

However, they succeed as such without the need for public sector subsidies or intervention from outside that bedevils other attempts: vouchers, community service schemes, 'twin moneys', or marginal employment subsidies to support socially useful work with a low or negative return on capital. A central reason for this is the willingness of members typically to price down their labour for local exchange.

This willingness is central to a vision of work organised and financed locally, for local production and exchange. This is a logical response to the globalised economy. It is hypocritical to call for protection or subsidy for British workers if those same workers intend to be global consumers.[3] But in a bounded, localised economic system, members give up claims to be global consumers and discover that they can be local producers. This is the principle of a 'multi-level' economy (Robertson, 1989).[4]

Richard Douthwaite, in a forthcoming book for the New Economics Foundation, explores from research across industrialised countries how such localised solutions can be made to work. For the benefits of reconnecting community, improving local quality of life and conviviality, creating local purchasing power and work, and building local environmental management, there may be an opportunity cost for those locally who can work or invest outside. As with LETS, where 'professionals' will accept less in local currency, investors placing their money in local social housing or a 'reinvestment trust' may not receive the same rate of return as outside. Community businesses accept that there is a potential trade-off between profit and employment creation, and consumers accept that local produce, such as food, may be more expensive (Douthwaite, 1995).[5] The non-monetary return is higher, the monetary return may not be.

Work for social gain

Localised approaches to work creation should be set within, rather than apart from, broader spheres of economic activity – the aim being greater self-reliance rather than autarchy. The social economy, which crosses from the local to the international, is also highly relevant as an example of practice.[6] This is for two reasons.

First, the social economy is also of particular relevance to deprived communities – having evolved a range of initiatives for a high-unemployment context. In addition, the social economy is itself a major provider of paid and unpaid work. London's formal voluntary sector, for example, comprises 30,000 organisations across the city. The voluntary sector in the USA, for example, is estimated by the corporate management guru, Peter Drucker, to be the country's largest single 'employer'.

Second, the more visionary leaders within the sector see their work as far more than alleviating the failures of market and state. They see it as offering an organising set of principles to refound the institutions of market and state on a social and ecological basis. The social economy therefore can be seen as a *demonstration* of a more sane and ecological economy, and hence of desirable patterns of work for the 21st century.

Work within the social economy is varied and should not be idealised, but can serve to *illustrate* work for social gain, through more inclusive and participative models of organisation,[7] greater recognition of the contribution of volunteering, explicit value-led motivation, and beneficial social or environmental impact.

This section assesses three aspects of work for social gain in the social economy: community enterprise, social investment and social entrepreneurs.

Community enterprise

Self-organisation is the key to work within the social economy (Benello *et al*, 1989). One example is community enterprise. This term includes a variety of co-operatives, community businesses, development trusts and community development corporations, which are established to provide work and meet social need in a financially viable way.[8] This is not for all forms of local work. Community enterprise is typically inappropriate for the sort of business more usually run as a sole trader or small partnership: window cleaning, television repairs, printing, wood stripping, jobbing, joinery.

However, since 1977, when the Highlands and Islands Development Board under Sir Kenneth Alexander set up its pioneering scheme to promote community enterprise in the high unemployment area of the Western Isles, community enterprise has in general proved to be a good way for people to:

- create and manage workspace, usually aimed at new-start enterprises and providing supportive advice, training and support infrastructure

- develop mixed-use properties and social housing

- run training programmes for local people

- run job-creation schemes

- offer local services, often on contract to the public sector

- run local commercial services, such as a village shop, which the private sector cannot make pay

- provide child-care services

- provide recreational facilities

- run local tourist/heritage centres

- provide specialist services to the wider social economy (Pearce, 1993).

Social investment: financing work for social gain

It has become widely agreed that the UK is a low-investment economy, and that long-term performance will require a rebalancing between investment and social consumption. Creating work in the local and social economy equally requires the channels for social investment. This is particularly true for micro-enterprises, co-operatives and community development trusts that have proved effective for work creation, but are poorly served by the mainstream financial services sector (Mayo, 1993).

Over recent years, the UK has seen a resurgence of interest in all forms of social investment. Associated with this has been the establishment, from a small base, of models of 'community banking' providing socially directed financial services. These range from credit unions, limited to the provision of savings and loans facilities for members, to more extended forms of development finance.

One of the best-known examples of these is South Shore Bank in Chicago. Established by ethical investors in 1973, South Shore Bank has used development loans to rehabilitate 28 per cent of its neighbourhood housing stock (population 78,000), with an average default rate of only 1.5 per cent (Shapiro, 1993). A first comparable UK model, the Aston Reinvestment Trust, has recently been established in Birmingham.

The success of South Shore Bank can be explained in part by the local dimension (its ability to reinvest local savings) and in part by the broader social economy dimension (its success in raising and leveraging finance from mainstream ethical investment funds outside).

Social entrepreneurship

LETS, community enterprise and social investment are illustrations of self- and community-organised work. A range of others exists. The conventional view that such social economy initiatives are pedestrian, low-risk ventures is simply wrong. Ironically, it is often in the 'Third World' more than here that the strength of local social and environmental innovation has been recognised. Key to this has been the role of social entrepreneurs. These are men and women who possess the entrepreneur's vision, creativity, forward-thinking and determination, but who devote these qualities to introducing and effecting innovative solutions to societal problems.

Most of organisational development work in the social economy focuses on effective leadership, so that there are many routes in which social economy leaders can receive training aimed at enhancing their performance. What is not yet well developed though are mechanisms for identifying and supporting potential leaders.

As with commercial entrepreneurs, the start-up phase of initiatives can be frustrated by many factors, such as the lack of support for the idea or the prior personal and institutional commitments of the social entrepreneur. Typically, the social entrepreneur then has to step outside existing institutions to find the freedom to launch an idea that will then change those institutions.

As a result, many potentially effective social innovations creating socially useful work do not come to fruition. This is particularly the case for those innovations that are being driven by disadvantaged people themselves, who are typically less articulate, less capable of constructing formal proposals, and less well connected to people with access to financial and other forms of support. There has traditionally been a far greater emphasis of this issue within the commercial sector. Many mechanisms exist to support 'start-up' phases of innovations with potential for commercial gain, ranging from public-sector-supported small business 'hothousing' programmes, through to corporate 'intrapreneuring', private investment fora and high-risk venture capital companies.

Lifeboats or armadas?

Such examples of work, at the local level and in the social economy, add up to a mosaic of emerging practice. They reflect the extent to which the traditional job is giving way to a variety of forms of productive activity – *fuzzy work* perhaps – which respond to a variety of social institutions, of which the classical labour market is only one. Self-employment at the margins is sweat equity and unpaid work, while unpaid volunteering is seen by many as a route to paid employment.

Rather than view work as waiting for an employer to offer a job, they point to the variety of ways in which, and social institutions through which, fulfilling work can be organised. Evolutionary institutional economics suggests that the concept of a 'labour market' is an unhelpful abstraction. What is important are the relevant institutions, and the context within which they operate. For conventional employment these may be firms, but for volunteering it may be volunteer agencies; for mutual exchange they may be the family or community.

At the same time, they clearly do *not* in themselves add up to a sufficient response to social need and environmental stress. At a time of high unemployment, environmental stress and in the face of the centrifugal forces of economic globalisation, they represent lifeboats: bootstrap ways of improving the quality of life and taking control. They could therefore also foreseeably form a minority part of a future scenario of work, which for the majority (in employment or out) is degrading and dependency-creating.

What will determine whether the lifeboats can become an armada, and form the basis for greater autonomy, social gain and environmental sustainability in the world of work, is therefore the broader political economy of policy change and shifting social morality. The key issues here are:

- What forms of income will be on offer for work that is unpaid?

- How will the benefits system change to promote desirable new work patterns?

- How is the environmental impact of work within society to become sustainable?

- What new work ethic will emerge to underpin these changes?

Social policy

Sustainable development
It is meaningless to consider the future of work outside the context of sustainable development. In crude terms, this is not the question 'do birds and bees work?' It is the question 'will there be work?'

While there is ongoing debate about the precise meaning of 'sustainable development', it is actually quite clear what needs to be done to reduce global and local environmental impacts: renewable resources must be renewed; the depletion of non-renewable resources must be accompanied by the development of renewable substitutes for them; wastes must be emitted no faster than they can safely be absorbed or neutralised by the environment; global environmental systems (climate, stratospheric ozone, biodiversity) must be protected; and risks should be kept within bounds set by the precautionary principle.

There is also little mystery about which economic sectors will need to be transformed for these conditions to be met: production and use of energy, industry, agriculture, and transport (Ekins, 1993). It is also clear that environmental policy does not necessarily cost jobs. In fact, 'defensive' expenditures – such as pollution abatement – are rising fast enough for some to talk of using the environmental crisis as a way of solving the unemployment crisis.

At present, two policy options dominate policy discussion in relation to sustainable development – both relevant to the world of work. The first are new indicators, which encompasses both social and environmental indicators. These are used to redefine wealth and progress, and redirect institutions and the economy towards broader social and environmental outcomes. The second is eco(logical/nomic)-tax reform.[9]

Over the last two decades in leading industrialised countries the proportion of public spending met through taxes on labour has increased, while taxes on capital have only increased slightly and those on natural resources have fallen (Belgian Bureau de Plan, 1994). This in itself offers a partial account of why there would be high unemployment.

Eco-tax reform, in short, shifts taxes off labour and business onto pollution and resource use. Green taxes reduce environmental externalities, but also allow for the reduction of distorting taxes such as those on labour. Such tax reform therefore provides a 'triple dividend': a more efficient fiscal system, reduced environmental externalities, and increased employment. This offers an effective route to employment creation by lowering the factor cost of labour, while doing so in a way that can be revenue-neutral for Government. Estimates of the net economic impact of one eco-tax reform proposal – the carbon energy tax coupled with a labour cost reduction – suggest that it could create 2,200,000 jobs in France, UK, Germany, Italy, Spain and Netherlands by 2010 (Belgian Bureau de Plan, 1994).

At the same time, it may be too optimistic to suggest that the shift towards environmental sustainability will change the overall context of high unemployment. And it will not all be win-win. Looking at estimates of environmental externalities for key sectors, for example, it is clear that four basic needs for poor households may need to rise in price over the coming decade: energy, food, water and transport. Although the Social Justice Commission simply ignored the environmental dimension, it is abundantly clear that issues of the environment and social justice are intricately linked.

Taxes and benefits
Do the concepts of 'full employment' and 'welfare state' go together – so that if we argue in favour of reconceiving work, we would argue for a reformed welfare state? One argument is yes, that if we do not return to full(er)

employment, the accrued financial costs of unemployment, in benefits and lost taxes, will settle the issue of whether there is to be welfare reform. There will have to be.

However, few proposals on the future of the welfare state come to terms with the changes in employment and work implied by no return to full employment. Recasting benefits as 'a springboard to employment' simply reinforces the walls of the social ghetto if there are not enough jobs to go round. The concept of 'full employability' popularised by Dahrendorf does the same if it assumes that there are somehow enough jobs for people to be employable for. The results offer unattractive and often socially divisive reforms (such as 'tough love') which deepen the confusion between a language of rights and a logic of rationing.

Such proposals reflect the adaptation of society to the flexible labour market. Good or bad, this process will happen sooner or later. But in maintaining the single goal of employment as the aim of welfare and training policies, they fail to address the full extent of dependency within, and exclusion from, that labour market.

If there is to be reform that is preferable to the present system, it needs to promote greater self-organisation and work for social gain, and provide, as Frank Field has argued, a basis for a clear, renewed social settlement that can command sufficient consensus and link those in and out of employment.

Self-organisation and work for social gain
The changes in work patterns identified in this chapter affect the 45-year-old man outside Doncaster who came out of the pits after closure of the coal mines, has health problems and may never be employed again, just as much as it does the 32-year-old London woman who works as a freelance consultant, travelling with the latest Charles Handy book tucked into her briefcase. But what is freedom for one may be dependency and insecurity for the other.

The policy agenda must therefore emphasise recreating forms of personal and social security in the face of such changes. One argument is that this should be the classic Beveridge idea of 'national insurance' reconstituted in a more meaningful form than now. Indeed, private income or mortgage-related insurance can certainly be expected to grow to allow for time out of paid work within the new, more flexible and uncertain work patterns. What is uncertain is whether relying on a state system of national insurance would be any more viable in financial terms in the long run and in the face of high unemployment than the current system.

A programme for self-reliance

A second approach is to set the idea of national insurance within a broader body of policy support for community and personal self-reliance. This programme for self-reliance would be based on guarantees of universal access to income, information and support, in the form of:

• special payments (supplementary to other benefits) for full-time carers

• guaranteed access to training, information, tools, materials and workshops to enable people to be able to be more self-reliant in clothing, shelter and food

• subsidies to registered community service organisations

• private or public sector forms of income insurance for short-term periods out of employment.

To take some examples, in the area of training, this implies shifting training and education from training for a job to training for not (necessarily) having a job. In the area of food, it implies promoting nutritional education and the uptake of allotments, permaculture and community-supported agriculture. In the area of health policy, it means working towards a health-promoting economy.

Such a programme could include traditional public sector work programmes, but rather than an emphasis on infrastructure development of uncertain benefit (repeated, for example, in the Delors White Paper), this should be on creative support directed through the social economy. In the USA, the Community Development Banking and Financial Institutions Act provides an important new model. The Act has established a Fund that will, in the name of community development and work creation, channel $382 million into the community banking sector by 1997 as equity grants, administrative grants, debt and technical assistance.

It will also require long-argued-for changes in national accounting to proceed in order for the wider social and environmental benefits of self-reliance to be accounted as more than a reduction in cash flows. Production (the single view of today's national accounts) is only one factor affecting the level of people's welfare. Others are health, employment, working conditions, (leisure) time, income distribution, scarce environmental goods (space, energy, natural resources, plant and animal species) and future security (Hueting, 1992). A more holistic set of national accounts will change the yardsticks by which politicians are judged and policy assessed.

Citizen's Income

The approach of a Citizen's Income offers, perhaps, a more complementary and more fundamental way to achieve such aims. A Citizen's Income would help to support beneficial changes in working patterns and practices by removing unemployment and poverty traps, eliminating today's black economy of undeclared earnings, raising pay levels for dirty and unsociable jobs, and encouraging work in the informal economy.

Yet at present there is enough evidence to suggest that a meaningful Citizen's Income cannot be financed out of income tax, and half a Citizen's Income offers at best a quarter of the argued benefits for it. This is where, rather than water down the Citizen's Income – the classic reform mentality – bold thinking is needed, looking at potential new taxes that could fund it.

The Eco-tax reform, discussed above, is one of the few desirable and feasible policies on the table centred on raising rather than spending large sums of money. Green taxes therefore open up the potential for a far more radical review of broader taxation and benefits policy.

One paper to take up this challenge is by James Robertson. He assesses the feasibility of combining four policy proposals: paying a Citizen's Income unconditionally to every citizen; abolishing taxes on incomes, profits and the value that is added by the production of useful goods and services; and replacing those taxes with a land-rent tax, and an energy tax (Robertson, 1994).

In recent years, support for each of the four of these proposals has grown. Robertson's work is the first to assess the feasibility and benefits of combining them, in a phased introduction over a minimum of 13 years. Energy taxes (falling on coal, oil, gas and nuclear power at the point of production), for example, have a strong constituency of support, but are by nature socially regressive, so that the progressive impact of the Citizen's Income is a complementary balance.

The implication is that negotiating small-step changes in the face of the sustainable development challenge simply creates new problems and that there is a need for a more open and radical debate within civil society, if we are to expect politicians to take it forward down the line. Even so, changes along these lines will take a long time to accomplish and may be more likely to happen as a muddled, piecemeal process of change – driven along by the pressure of events and developing public awareness – than as a coherent long-term public policy programme.

Social morality

A new work ethic?

The underlying 'settlement' reflected by the policy proposals discussed above is that:

1. Taxes should be levied where value is being subtracted from the common good (such as pollution), and not where value is being added (such as work and enterprise). This is a shift from taxing value-added (such as VAT) to taxing value-subtracted (VST).

2. All citizens should have an adequate income and be able to use their labour and talents for themselves and for the common good.

3. There should be a fairer deal between women and men in terms of income and different forms of work, and a better start for children, in families and communities better able to protect themselves from the social disintegration associated with economic globalisation.

4. The key functions of the biosphere should be protected and consumption of energy and materials in industrialised countries reduced.

Yet alongside these principles is the need for a social morality which will complement the desirable changes in practice and policy needed. The traditional 'work ethic' has underpinned the rise of employment over the last two hundred years. At the same time, in establishing employment with society's imprimatur as the principal source of personal identity and means of social participation, it has helped to reinforce social exclusion and the lack of self-worth associated with unemployment.

More recently, the 'market ethic' has elevated individual self-interest into a reigning dogma. This has also helped to devalue and erode unpaid work in the form of non-market institutions such as the family and community, which have traditionally performed many of the tasks of community support and mutual care.

Finally, the 'consumer ethic' has defined what makes for the good life in society – offering surrogate fulfilment through packaged leisure, fashion and consumer goods. The extent to which leisure fails to provide for fulfilment is noted in Mihaly Csikszentmihalyi's work *Flow: The Psychology of Happiness*. Overwork for overconsumption is environmentally catastrophic. It is also socially divisive, as individualistic consumption means that landscapes are carved up by single housing units and single-occupant transport. A single UK consumer, with a car used perhaps 4 per cent of the time and short-life consumer durables in the household, keeps opportunities of consumption on stock that would suffice for the supply of whole villages in Africa.

In their own ways, therefore, the 'work', 'market' and 'consumer' ethics have all helped to undermine personal autonomy and social cohesion. Where conventional labour market economists talk of the power of 'insiders' and 'outsiders' in the labour market, the underlying message is that the UK no longer has the social cohesion needed to share working income or working time.

As a result, policies such as sharing working time, increased social legislation to reduce hours and enforce rights to time out, or taxation of work over 40 hours a week, find it hard to get a full hearing in the UK. Without a new 'social contract' only force can make those out of employment take jobs that do not pay enough to live on, or make those in jobs give up working time and income to those out of employment.

No account of work should leave aside the issue of consumption and wasted leisure. It is remarkable that capitalism, which has socialised labour and made it extremely productive, has produced the most individualistic and unproductive consumption (Reifner, 1995).

But alongside this, there is a need to evolve a new work ethic that does not penalise unpaid work of social benefit and fits with more flexible and autonomous patterns of work within society. In the language of rights and responsibilities, Paul Ekins (1993) describes the new ethics as a twin proposition linking rights to and responsibilities for both paid and unpaid work:

- Everyone has a right to paid work and to access to the necessary resources (skills, land, workshops) to enable them to do unpaid work for themselves, their families and communities.

- Everyone has a responsibility to work according to their abilities, both to generate wealth corresponding to the goods and services they consume, and to contribute to the society which guarantees them, among other things, the right to work.

In more poetic terms, Shann Turnbull (1975) describes this as:

from each according to his interest;
to each according to his contribution;
provided the basic needs of all are fulfilled.

So, returning to the quotation at the very start of this chapter, we should recall that what we need is a system of work, in which, instead of believing in a job, people can believe in themselves.

Notes

1. One of a series of 'personal perspectives' presented at a conference on 'Work, Wealth and Worth' in 1993 in North-East England, organised by Respond! One outcome of the conference was a project to explore how, with or without a job, one's sense of self-worth can be rediscovered through a broader understanding of what work and wealth is, both to communities and to society.

2. The subject of a New Economics Foundation/Joseph Rowntree Charitable Trust project at present.

3. A point I owe to Paul Ekins.

4. Such principles, at the same time, are not necessarily new. Present day ideas and action models such as community land trusts, the integration of town and country ('villages of co-operation'), LETS ('national equitable labour exchanges'), permaculture ('no dig agriculture') and community schools ('halls of science') were all linked activities within the 19th century Owenite movement (Conaty, 1994). From the Worgl experimentation with negative-interest monies to the Austral regional currencies in Argentina, there is an unwritten history of such community economics. At a time when building societies are embracing conventional banking forms, such history is perhaps of particular relevance.

5. This makes it clear that localised solutions will be prey to market predators from outside. The under-capitalised food co-operative will compete with the commercial discount store ready to take losses if it can drive out competition. Credit unions will compete with commercial banks as well as licensed money lenders. At the same time, there is evidence to suggest that businesses are withdrawing rapidly from low-income areas, led by the commercial banks (Mayo, 1993). Furthermore, social economy initiatives trade on more than price and consumer choice (where they too may be

competitive) – drawing successfully on the community 'goodwill' of customer loyalty, investor values and volunteer support.

6. A word on definitions, of which there are many for the 'social economy', none final as all economic activity has a social dimension. The least helpful are those that import an institutional breakdown from elsewhere. My view is that it is helpful to use inclusive rather than exclusive terms, and that the two core characteristics of the sector are 'economic activities that embody an intentional orientation towards social gain' (Zadek and Mansell, 1995) and a growing sense of identity as a new sector of the economy which, rather than being dependent on the 'wealth-creating' lead sectors of the traded economy, is in itself a (or even the) major contributor to social wealth and welfare. The social economy is not merely a provider of 'tradeables' or 'non-tradeables', it is a critical and substantial part of the fabric of life for all.

7. Although the voluntary sector still lacks an appropriate language of organisation with which to describe itself. The flood of management thinking which penetrated the sector in the 1980s stressed narrow conceptions of efficiency, motivation and structure, which are now viewed as flawed within the corporate sector. Ironically, the corporate sector is now moving towards a model that typifies many social economy initiatives.

8. As with other social economy initiatives, to achieve this requires a more sophisticated form of accounting than return on capital. So one of the most important recent developments in the field is the emergence of an agreed schematic approach to do this – the social audit – which captures the broader social and environmental costs and benefits.

9. Both advocated in the UK by the New Economics Foundation since its inception.

References

Belgian Bureau de Plan (1994) *Tax Reform and Sustainable Development*, Discussion paper for the European Commission, reprinted in *Europe Environment*, supplement February 1995

Benello, G., Swann, R. and Turnbull, S. (1989) *Building Sustainable Communities: Tools and Concepts for Self-reliant Economic Change*, TOES, New York

Bridges, W. (1995) *Jobshift*, Nicholas Brealy, London

Chambers, R. (1995) *Poverty and Livelihood: Whose Reality Counts?* IDS Discussion Paper 347, Brighton

Conaty, P. (1994) 'Back to the future', *New Economics*, Winter 1994, London

Csikszentmihalyi, M. (1992) *Flow: The Psychology of Happiness*, Harper and Row, London

Douthwaite, R. (1995, forthcoming) *Short Circuit*, New Economics Foundation

EcoConcern (1995) *Innovative Proposals for Re-thinking the Economy*, Barcelona

Ekins, P. (1993) *Recovering Sustainably,* Paper presented to a New Economics Foundation seminar 'Green Routes to Recovery', London

Glendinning, H. and McLaughlin, E. (1993) *Paying for Care: Lessons from Europe*, SSAC, HMSO, London

Gorz, A. (1982) *Farewell to the Working Class*, Pluto Press, London

Griffiths, J. (1995) *Business and Social Exclusion*, Report to London Enterprise Agency conference

Handy, C. (1989) *The Age of Unreason*, Business Books, London

Hueting, R. (1992) in P. Ekins and M. Max-Neef (eds) *Real-Life Economics*, Routledge, London

Lane, R. (1993) *The Market Experience*, University Press

Mayo, E. (ed.) (1993) *BankWatch*, New Economics Foundation, London

Pahl, R. (1984) *Divisions of Labour*, Blackwell, Oxford

Pearce, J. (1993) *At the Heart of the Community Economy*, Calouste Gulbenkian, London

Reifner, U. (1995) Personal Correspondence to John Turner

Robertson, J. (1991) *Future Wealth: A New Economics for the 21st Century*, Cassells, London

Robertson, J. (1994) *Taxes and Benefits*, New Economics Foundation, London

Robertson, J. (1995) *Electronics, Environment and Employment*, Green College, Oxford

Shapiro, J. (1993) *The Business of Development Banking*, Paper presented at Financial Empowerment conference, Loccum, Germany

Sparkes, R. (1995) *The Ethical Investor*, London

Thomas, J.J. (1992) *Informal Economic Activity*, Harvester Wheatsheaf, Hemel Hempstead

Turnbull, S. (1975) *Money Sources and Profit Motives*, Company Directors' Association, Sydney

Zadek, S. (1993) *An Economics of Utopia*, Avebury, Aldershot

Zadek, S. and Mansell, R. (1995) *The Social Economy of Telematics*, unpublished paper, New Economics Foundation, Science Policy Research Unit